Copyright © 2024 by Camille Hanson – Learn English with Camille
Editor: Christine Irvine – Instagram: Facts about English
Cover Art & Layout: Calvin Hanson – CH Creative

All rights reserved. No part of this book may be reproduced in any form without permission in writing from the publisher/authors, except in the case of brief quotations in articles, blogs, or reviews.

For permissions: books@learnenglishwithcamille.com

Contents

1. Flash Flood — 3
2. College Dilemma — 8
3. Young and in Love — 14
4. Job Search — 20
5. Choosing to Live in Portugal — 26
6. Adopting a Baby — 32
7. Scammed — 37
8. Root Canal — 43
9. Speeding Ticket — 48
10. Rollerblading Mishaps — 54
11. Beginning College — 60
12. Restored Hope — 66
13. Rollerblading in Barcelona — 71
14. A Surprise Guest — 76
15. Bitten by a Weever Fish — 81
16. The Coolest Babysitter — 87

17. Our BEST day in Italy	92
18. A Day at Sea	97
19. The Bet	102
20. Snow	107
21. Learning How to Make Sourdough	112
22. The BEST Breakfast We've Ever Had	117
23. Starting Learn English with Camille	123
24. A Brazilian Christmas	129
25. I Made the Tabloids in Peru	134
26. Caught	140
27. My First Job	145
28. Embarrassing Moment	150
29. Our Worst EVER Airbnb guests	155
30. A Date to Remember	160
31. Answer Key	165

ADVANCED ENGLISH (B2-C1)

ENGLISH
Short Stories

30 Short Stories Written For Advanced English Learners

How to use this book

This is a book of advanced level short stories. Most of them are 300-400 words and written with real life English words and phrases. I wrote these stories as if I were writing them to a friend. More than half of these stories are 100% true, and some of them are fiction. There is a note by the title, so you can know if it's true or not.

Learning English through stories is an amazing way to advance in your language learning journey. You will improve your vocabulary and grammar all while having fun. Read each story. Highlight any new words. Don't worry about trying to understand every single word. Try to understand the main ideas. At the end of every story, there is a word list with definitions and a multiple choice quiz. Answers can be found in the back of the book.

Be sure to listen to the free audio that accompanies each story. Read the stories as many times as you would like. Use the note section in the back of the book to practice writing your own short stories in English.

As always, happy learning.

Get your FREE audiobook download!

Go to the END of STORY 9

NOTE: This is so Amazon Preview viewers can't download free audio. I appreciate your support and for learning with me! ~ Camille

One

Flash Flood

TRUE STORY

We were in Denizli, Türkiye with my dear content creator friend Janet and her husband Ramazan. They had made dinner reservations at a nice restaurant just about 30 minutes away from their house. It was early evening, and we were on our way to the restaurant with two of our kids. Our oldest son stayed home because he was feeling a little under the weather. Calvin happened to be driving, so we picked up Ramazan from work on our way to the restaurant.

Suddenly, it started to rain. It started raining harder, and water started flowing down the street. Our windshield wipers were on full blast, but we could barely see. Cars were pulling over to wait for the storm to pass. We decided to do the same. The rain wouldn't let up. It was a torrential downpour. Before we knew it, it was like a river on the street. We saw flip-flops, a garbage can, balls, and trash all floating down the street. What was happening?! We didn't know if our car was going to float away too. We could see people filming the chaos out of their shop windows.

There was a moment where I actually felt nervous. I didn't want to show it because I didn't want my kids to worry. I wished our other son was with us. All we could do was wait and pray. We had been parked for over an hour when the storm finally seemed to let up a little bit. We decided to back up and go back home a different way. Luckily, we made it home. It turns out the street we were on got hit the hardest. Janet and Ramazan said they had never experienced anything like that in all their years in Türkiye. We were thankful they were in the car with us. That was the first and hopefully the last flash flood we will ever have to experience.

◆◆◆◆◆◆◆◆◆◆◆◆◆◆◆◆◆◆◆◆◆◆◆◆◆◆◆◆◆◆◆◆

Word List

content creator (**noun**) - someone who creates content

under the weather (**idiom**) - feeling sick, not 100% well. Sometimes it can mean a slight cold.

pick up (**phrasal verb**) - to increase intensity

windshield wiper (**noun**) - the part of the car with a rubber blade and an arc that moves to keep the windshield clear of rain

full blast (**idiom**) - maximum power or intensity

pull over (**phrasal verb**) - to move to the side of the road

torrential (**adjective**) - used to refer to very heavy rain

downpour (**noun**) - heavy rainfall

let up (phrasal verb) - to stop or become slower

hit (verb) - to affect

flash flood (noun) - a sudden local flood

Multiple Choice Quiz

1. What were the dinner plans for the evening in Denizli?
A) A picnic in the park
B) Dinner at a friend's house
C) Dinner reservations at a restaurant
D) Takeout from a local café

2. Why did the family pull over on their way to the restaurant?
A) Their car broke down.
B) They needed directions.
C) There was heavy rain and poor visibility.
D) They needed to pick up a friend.

3. Who was driving the car during the storm?
A) Calvin
B) Ramazan
C) Janet
D) The oldest son

4. Where was Ramazan?

A) At work

B) At home

C) Waiting at the restaurant

D) Out shopping

5. What items did they see floating in the flooded street?

A) Books and notebooks

B) Flip-flops, a garbage can, balls, and trash

C) Umbrellas and raincoats

D) Toys and board games

6. How long were they parked during the storm?

A) 30 minutes

B) Over an hour

C) 15 minutes

D) 45 minutes

7. What made Camille feel nervous during the storm?

A) The thunder

B) The wind

C) The rising flood water

D) The darkness

8. Why wasn't their oldest son with them during the storm?

A) He was sleeping.

B) He was too tired to go.

C) He was feeling under the weather.

D) He was at a friend's house.

9. How did they eventually make it home?
A) They swam.
B) They waited for the storm to pass.
C) They drove back the same way.
D) They found a different route.

10. How did Janet and Ramazan react to the flash flood?
A) They were calm and experienced.
B) They were excited and took pictures.
C) They were very surprised.
D) They were indifferent and continued their journey.

Two

College Dilemma

Heather had pulled two all-nighters, and she was exhausted. She could barely keep her eyes open, but if she didn't pass these exams, her mom would kill her. She was a sophomore this year, but she had spent a little too much time partying and not enough time studying. She knew it was wrong, but she couldn't help herself. She was part of the in-crowd, and she liked it. It was much different from high school where no one acknowledged her existence.

She was majoring in finance but was thinking of changing her major. Her guidance counselor said that Heather should change her major by next semester if she still wanted to graduate on time. The problem was she didn't know what she really wanted to study. Did she really have to decide what she wanted to do for the rest of her life at the age of 20? Her parents wanted her to stay in finance because it had a promising future. Her dad was a bank manager, and Heather could easily get a job at his bank if she wanted one. Of course her dad wanted her to follow in his footsteps, but he didn't pressure her.

Heather knew she wanted to get a bachelor's degree, and she was planning on spending a semester abroad. She hoped it would be in France so that she could keep studying French. She was at a basic conversational level, and she knew she had a long way to go. Her parents weren't thrilled about her plans to study abroad, but she knew deep down that she had their support. Having never left the USA, her parents couldn't wrap their heads around why she would want to spend time in another country. They were worried for her safety. She was their only child.

Heather started tossing around the idea of studying business and also linguistics. She needed to focus on studying, so she made a mental note to see her guidance counselor next week. She quickly downed another espresso and opened up her economics book. She knew it was going to be another long night.

Word List

pull an all-nighter (idiom) - to stay up all night (usually to study)

kill someone (expression) - to be very mad at someone

sophomore (noun) - a student in the second year of high school or college

couldn't help herself (idiom) - unable to control her actions; unable to stop herself from doing something

in-crowd (noun) - the popular kids, often athletes

major in (**phrasal verb**) - to have a specified subject as your main subject of study

semester (**noun**) - one of two usually 18-week periods that make up an academic year at a college or university

graduate (**verb**) - to finish school

bachelor's degree (**noun**) - a four year degree at a college or university

semester abroad (**noun**) - semester of college or university in another country

thrilled (**adjective**) - very excited and happy

wrap your head around (**something**) (**idiom**) - to find a way to understand or accept (something)

toss around (**phrasal verb**) - consider something as an option

make a mental note (**phrase**) - remind yourself to do something in your head

follow in someone's footsteps (**idiom**) - to do the same thing someone else did previously, especially as a job

down (**verb**) - quickly drink

◆◆◆◆◆◆◆◆◆◆◆◆◆◆◆◆◆◆◆◆◆◆◆◆◆◆◆◆◆◆◆◆◆

Multiple Choice Quiz

1. Why is Heather exhausted in the story?
A) She had a busy day at work.
B) She had pulled two all-nighters.
C) She was traveling.
D) She was sick.

2. What consequences will Heather face if she doesn't pass her exams?
A) She will be grounded.
B) She will lose her place in college.
C) Her mom will be disappointed.
D) She will get kicked off the volleyball team.

3. What is Heather's major in college?
A) Linguistics
B) Business
C) Finance
D) Economics

4. Why is Heather considering changing her major?
A) She dislikes finance.
B) She doesn't know what she wants to study.
C) Her guidance counselor suggested it.
D) She wants to travel abroad.

5. Why does Heather hope to spend a semester abroad in France?
A) To party in a different country
B) To improve her French language skills
C) To escape her parents
D) To find a new major

6. How do Heather's parents feel about her studying abroad?
A) Thrilled
B) Worried for her safety
C) Indifferent
D) Angry and disappointed

7. What is Heather's current level of proficiency in French?
A) Fluent
B) Basic
C) Intermediate
D) Advanced

8. Why do Heather's parents want her to stay in finance?
A) Because they are both bankers
B) Because it has a promising future
C) Because they dislike linguistics
D) Because Heather's dad is a linguist

9. What does Heather plan to discuss with her guidance counselor next week?
A) Changing her major
B) Studying abroad
C) Her parents' concerns
D) Joining a party club

10. What did Heather drink before facing a long night of studying?
A) Red Bull
B) Soda
C) Espresso
D) Black tea

Three

Young and in Love

Isabel couldn't stop thinking about Hayden. They had only been on three dates, but she was already smitten. He was so handsome with his piercing green eyes and his curly brown locks. She couldn't wait to see him again. They had recently made plans to go sledding. She loved that they actually did activities together. Hayden was so outdoorsy; it was something they had in common.

Hayden was a foreign exchange student from Sweden. Isabel couldn't believe that out of all the girls in school, Haden had chosen her to spend time with. They met because of their assigned seats in science class. They had to spend an hour every afternoon dissecting frogs and mixing chemicals in beakers. Science quickly became Isabel's favorite class.

She hadn't told her parents about Hayden yet because they wouldn't let her date until she was 16. Her 16th birthday was only three weeks away, so she figured she might as well wait until then. Only her sister Claire knew, but Isabel had sworn Claire to secrecy. Claire promised that she would take Isabel's secret to the grave.

Isabel's phone beeped and startled her out of her daydream. She glanced down to see a message that said, "See you at River Hill in 15. H." She quickly threw on her snow pants, boots, and jacket. She grabbed her hat, mittens, and scarf. River Hill was just a five-minute walk from her house. She and Hayden had planned on sledding for an hour and then wanted to drink the world's best hot chocolate at Elsa's Cafe. Isabel hoped Elsa would have her freshly baked gooey chocolate chip cookies. Last time she went to the cafe, they were sold out.

Isabel could see Hayden from a distance, so she picked up her pace. Her heart always skipped a beat when she saw him. He saw her, and a huge grin broke out on his face. Those dimples!

"I'm one lucky girl," Isabel thought. She didn't want to think about the end of the school year when Hayden would go back to Sweden. She was already planning to see if she could study there. But for now, she planned to enjoy every minute possible with Hayden.

Hayden had his red sled tucked under his arm. "Let's ride," he told her excitedly.

"I feel like I'm already on a ride," Isabel chuckled to herself. "Let's go!" she responded, matching his energy.

◆◆◆◆◆◆◆◆◆◆◆◆◆◆◆◆◆◆◆◆◆◆◆◆◆◆◆◆◆◆◆◆

Word List

date (noun) - romantic outing

smitten (**adjective**) - in love with someone or something

sled (**verb**) - to ride on a sled, especially down a hill

foreign exchange student (**noun**) - a student who comes from another country to study

assigned seat (**noun**) - a seat you are told to sit in

dissect (**verb**) - to take something apart often in an effort to learn more about it

beaker (**noun**) - glass containers used to mix something, often chemicals

swear to secrecy (**idiom**) - to make someone promise to keep a secret

take a secret to the grave (**idiom**) - never tell anyone

daydream (**noun**) - pleasant thoughts that distract you from the present moment

snow pants (**noun**) - pants worn in the snow to keep you dry

mitten (**noun**) - a covering for your hand in cold weather that has a separate part for the thumb

gooey (**adjective**) - soft and sticky

heart skips a beat (**idiom**) - you feel nervous or excited about something

grin (**noun**) - a big smile

dimple (noun) - a small area on a part of a person's body (such as the cheek or chin) that naturally curves in

◆◆◆◆◆◆◆◆◆◆◆◆◆◆◆◆◆◆◆◆◆◆◆◆◆◆◆◆

Multiple Choice Quiz

1. How does Isabel describe Hayden's physical appearance?
A) Average
B) Unattractive
C) Handsome with piercing green eyes and curly brown locks
D) Blond with blue eyes

2. How many dates have Isabel and Hayden been on?
A) One
B) Two
C) Three
D) Four

3. What activity did Isabel and Hayden plan for their next meeting?
A) Watching a movie
B) Going sledding
C) Visiting a museum
D) Having a picnic

4. How did Isabel and Hayden meet?

A) Through mutual friends

B) In a science class

C) At a party

D) During a school assembly

5. Why did science become Isabel's favorite class?

A) She loved dissecting frogs.

B) She enjoyed mixing chemicals in beakers.

C) Hayden was in the same class.

D) It was an easy class.

6. When is Isabel's 16th birthday?

A) Two weeks away

B) Three weeks away

C) Four weeks away

D) Five weeks away

7. Who is the only person Isabel has told about dating Hayden?

A) Her parents

B) Her best friend

C) Her sister Claire

D) Her science teacher

8. Where did Hayden suggest meeting Isabel for sledding?

A) River Hill

B) Elsa's Cafe

C) School courtyard

D) Isabel's house

9. What treat does Isabel hope is at the cafe?
A) Ice cream
B) Fresh baked gooey chocolate chip cookies
C) Pie
D) Cupcakes

10. How does Isabel feel about Hayden leaving at the end of the school year?
A) Indifferent
B) Excited for the future
C) Worried and already planning to visit Sweden
D) Happy to have some time alone

Four

Job Search

Alex had graduated college just over a year ago. He was currently an intern at a local radio station, but it was an unpaid position, and he needed money. He wanted to move out of his parents' house and start his own life. His parents weren't pressuring him, but it was one of his personal goals. Also, his three younger brothers were all still living at home, and Alex wanted space. He was going to be 24 years old next month, so he felt it was time for him to move; however, he needed to find a paying job first.

Alex had sent out ten job applications over the last two months, but none of the companies had responded to his applications. The current job market was tough. He had experience working in radio, and he was interested in being a TV host. Every morning he scanned the online ads, searching for jobs. He also signed up on LinkedIn in an effort to broaden his network. "These things take time. Be patient," his mom's voice echoed in his head. Maybe his mom was right.

Alex clicked refresh on his email and saw one new message. He clicked on it and skimmed through it: *paid intern, one year,* and *New*

York were words that caught his attention. He read through the email more thoroughly. It turns out his boss had heard about a new TV show that was looking for a potential host. The show wasn't starting for six more months, but they were looking for someone to intern to learn the ropes as the show was preparing to launch. The pay wasn't bad, but it meant moving to New York. Not only that, but the job started next week! Alex couldn't believe it. He wasn't a city boy; he was from a small fishing village in Maine. He decided to talk to his family and his current boss about the opportunity.

His boss encouraged him to take the leap. "I spent five years in New York, and it was definitely a growing experience. Go with your gut, son."

"It seems like a promising opportunity," his mom said.

Alex decided to sleep on it. The next morning, he wrote out a huge list of pros and cons. The pros far outweighed the cons. He replied to the initial email saying that he was very interested in the internship. The company responded within an hour asking to interview him over a video call. Alex was so nervous, but he quickly showered and got ready, mentally rehearsing what he was going to say. The interview went so smoothly that it almost seemed too good to be true. But it was true. They offered him the job, and he accepted the offer, immediately starting to pack his suitcase. He only had a few loose ends to tie up with his current job, and he was thrilled for this new adventure.

Word List

intern (noun) - a student or trainee who works to gain experience (sometimes unpaid)

goal (noun) - something that you are trying to achieve

tough (adjective) - difficult

scan (verb) - to quickly look over something

ad (noun) - advertisement

skim (verb) - to look over or read (something) quickly especially to find the main ideas

learn the ropes (idiom) - to learn how something works

launch (verb) - to start something

city boy (noun) - someone who enjoys the city

take a leap (idiom) - to go for something; to do something risky or uncertain

go with your gut (idiom) - go with what you feel is right

promising (adjective) - likely to succeed or be good

sleep on (phrasal verb) - to delay making a decision about something until the following day

outweigh (**verb**) - to be greater or more significant than something else

mentally rehearse (**expression**) - to think deeply and repeatedly about what you're going to say

loose end (**noun**) - a detail that isn't yet settled

tie up (**phrasal verb**) - to settle; to deal with something in order to complete something

Multiple Choice Quiz

1. What is Alex's current job at the beginning of the story?
A) TV host
B) Radio station intern
C) Unemployed
D) Office assistant

2. Why does Alex want to find a paying job?
A) To buy a new car
B) To move out of his parents' house
C) To travel the world
D) To support his younger brothers

3. What is Alex's interest besides working in radio?

A) Writing novels

B) Acting

C) Being a TV host

D) Graphic design

4. How many younger brothers does Alex have?

A) One

B) Two

C) Three

D) Four

5. Where is Alex originally from?

A) New York

B) Maine

C) California

D) Florida

6. What catches Alex's attention in the job offer?

A) High salary

B) One-year contract

C) Unpaid internship

D) Remote work opportunity

7. What does Alex's boss advise him to do when Alex considers the New York opportunity?

A) Stay in the current job

B) Take the leap and go to New York

C) Find a different internship

D) Focus on radio, not TV hosting

8. How does Alex's mom respond to his opportunity?
A) She is stressed.
B) She is unpleasant.
C) She is positive.
D) She discourages him.

9. What does Alex do after receiving the job offer email?
A) Rejects the offer
B) Sleeps on it
C) Ignores the email
D) Accepts the offer immediately

10. How does the video interview for the New York opportunity go for Alex?
A) It is a disaster.
B) It is smooth and almost too good to be true.
C) Alex doesn't show up.
D) It is interrupted by technical issues.

Five

Choosing to Live in Portugal

True story

We had been traveling for eight months, and we were tired. We had burned ourselves out. We always get so excited about traveling, but then we do too much; we visit too many cities and see too many sights. We had no desire to travel any more, but we didn't want to go back to the US. Yes, we missed our family and friends there, but we come alive when we're overseas, like we're fulfilling part of our purpose in life.

We had always dreamed of living in Europe and having a European passport. We love the sea and historical cities. There weren't too many countries where we could apply for a visa while residing in that country. Many countries would require us to travel back to the US to apply for a visa. We were drawn to Portugal because we could apply for residency while already living in the country, and we could join their tax program, which offered many benefits. We also both speak Portuguese (though Brazilian), so it was a good head start. After thinking and praying about it for a few weeks, we decided to take a huge leap of faith. We didn't know anyone in Portugal, but we found a beautiful Airbnb, and we rented it for a month. The host turned out to be amazing and very helpful.

When we decided to apply for Portuguese visas, we randomly chose a lawyer online because we felt too overwhelmed doing the whole process ourselves. It turned out to be the best decision ever. The lawyer helped us open a bank account, apply for the tax program, submit all of our documents, and connect us with a realtor who found us an amazing house to rent. The house happened to be in a small beach town an hour north of Porto. It has a yard with a small pool and many fruit trees. My favorite room is a porch that has huge windows overlooking both the town and the sea. It's honestly better than we could have ever imagined. We're able to walk to the city center in ten minutes.

We're only two months into living here in Portugal, but so far every day I have woken up grateful and feeling so blessed. We're living a life that we had previously only dreamed of. Maybe I'm still in the honeymoon stage. I don't know what the future holds, but I hope it's many years here in Portugal. We know that we will eventually recover from travel burnout, but we're hoping that we can make Portugal our home.

◆◆◆◆◆◆◆◆◆◆◆◆◆◆◆◆◆◆◆◆◆◆◆◆◆◆◆◆◆◆◆◆◆

Word List

burn out (phrasal verb) - to get extremely tired of doing something

come alive (idiom) - to become excited and energetic

historical (adjective) - very old

visa (noun) - a document required to enter/stay in some countries

reside (verb) - to live in a particular place

be drawn to (idiom) - to be attracted to something or someone

head start (noun) - an advantage over something

benefit (noun) - an advantage or profit gained from something

leap of faith (idiom) - to step into the unknown with faith

Airbnb (noun) - an online platform used by people who want to rent out their home or by customers who want to stay in someone's home

randomly (adverb) - happens by chance more than by plan

overwhelmed (adjective) - feeling that there is too much going on for you to handle by yourself

porch (noun) - a covered shelter connected to a house

honeymoon stage (noun) - the beginning phase of something where everything is fun and exciting

eventually (adverb) - at an unspecified later time; in the end

Multiple Choice Quiz

1. How long had Camille and her family been traveling before feeling tired and burned out?

A) 6 months

B) 8 months

C) 10 months

D) 12 months

2. Why didn't they want to return to the US, despite missing family and friends?

A) They preferred European culture.

B) They felt more alive overseas.

C) They had a job opportunity in Europe.

D) They were avoiding travel restrictions.

3. What aspect of Europe did Camille and her family always dream of?

A) The mountains

B) Having a European passport

C) The countryside

D) Traveling in Europe

4. Why were Camille and her partner drawn to Portugal?

A) They had family there.

B) They spoke Portuguese.

C) They found a job opportunity.

D) They loved Portuguese cuisine.

5. What benefit does Portugal offer that influenced their decision to move there?
A) A discount on travel expenses
B) Access to a tax program with benefits
C) Free language lessons
D) Opportunities for social events

6. How did Camille and her family find accommodation in Portugal?
A) Through a recommendation from a friend
B) Randomly picking an Airbnb
C) Booking a hotel online
D) Staying with a local family

7. Why did they decide to hire a lawyer for the residency process?
A) They didn't trust the online process.
B) The lawyer was a family friend.
C) They felt overwhelmed doing it themselves.
D) The lawyer was recommended by a friend.

8. What was part of the lawyer's role in the process of settling in Portugal?
A) Finding a job
B) Opening a bank account
C) Booking flights
D) Planning tourist activities

9. Where is the house they rented located?
A) In the city center of Porto
B) An hour north of Porto in a small beach town
C) In the countryside
D) In the mountains

10. How does the family feel about living in Portugal after two months?
A) Regretful
B) Tired and burned out
C) Grateful and blessed
D) Hesitant and unsure

Six

Adopting a Baby

Miram and Scott couldn't have been more excited. After years of trying to have a baby, they finally decided to take the route of adoption. They had filled out all their forms and had their home inspection; now they were just waiting for a call. They had been waiting for six months to be exact.

When the phone rang one Saturday afternoon, Miriam had a feeling this was it, the moment she had been waiting for. She wasn't disappointed. It was the adoption agency asking if they could fly to Phoenix tomorrow because a baby girl was about to be born. The mother of the baby girl was young; she was only 18 years old and she felt like she couldn't commit to raising a baby all on her own. She had searched through all the potential adoptive parents and finally settled on Miriam and Scott. She was drawn to their kind smiles and warm eyes.

"Phoenix? Tomorrow? Yes, yes, we will be there," Miriam replied.

Miriam and Scott found a red-eye flight leaving in six hours, so they started to pack their bags. Miriam took extra care to pack her carefully chosen baby outfits, pacifiers, and bottles. She couldn't believe the moment had finally arrived. They quickly texted their families to tell them the news, and Miriam's mother agreed to watch their Cocker Spaniel while they were away.

The flight went smoothly, and when the plane landed, Miriam and Scott went straight to the hospital. They were in the waiting room when a nurse called their names and told them they could go back to meet their new baby. They had already settled on the name Elise, meaning God's promise. When they saw Elise, she was even more perfect than they could have ever imagined. She already had a head full of hair and chubby little legs.

The young mother looked exhausted but thankful as she handed Elise over to Miriam. "I know you will take care of her," she said tearfully.

"Oh we will. Thank you so much for giving us this precious gift. You have no idea how much she means to us," Miriam responded, also crying. As Miriam held her baby for the first time, she had such a wave of emotion wash over her, but gratitude was the strongest. She smiled as her gaze met her daughter's for the very first time.

◆◆◆◆◆◆◆◆◆◆◆◆◆◆◆◆◆◆◆◆◆◆◆◆◆◆◆◆◆◆

Word List

adoption (**noun**) - the act of legally taking someone's biological child and raising it as your own

home inspection (noun) - a safety and quality assessment of your home

settle on (phrasal verb) - to choose after thinking of other possible choices

Phoenix (noun) - the capital of Arizona, a state in the United States

red-eye flight (noun) - an overnight flight arriving the next morning at its destination

pacifier (noun) - a rubber teat for a baby to suck on

Cocker Spaniel (noun) - a small breed of dog

chubby (adjective) - somewhat fat (usually used with babies)

gaze (noun) - a steady intent look

Multiple Choice Quiz

1. Why were Scott and Miriam excited?
A) They were going on vacation.
B) They were adopting a baby.
C) They had just moved to a new city.
D) They had adopted a pet.

2. How did Scott and Miriam decide to start a family?
A) Through natural conception
B) By undergoing fertility treatments
C) Through adoption
D) By fostering children

3. Why did the birth mother choose Scott and Miriam for adoption?
A) They lived in Phoenix.
B) They had warm eyes and kind smiles.
C) They were wealthy.
D) They were related to her.

4. What was the name they had already chosen for the baby?
A) Emily
B) Ella
C) Elise
D) Emma

5. How did Miriam feel when she received the call from the adoption agency?
A) Disappointed
B) Excited
C) Annoyed
D) Relieved

6. How did they travel to Phoenix for the adoption?
A) By car
B) By train
C) By red-eye flight
D) By bus

7. Who agreed to watch their pet while they were away?

A) Miriam's mother

B) Scott's brother

C) A neighbor

D) Miriam's friend

8. What did Miriam pack for the baby?

A) Toys

B) Diapers

C) Carefully chosen baby outfits, pacifiers, and bottles

D) Books

9. What does Elise mean?

A) Bright and shining

B) God's promise

C) Princess

D) Joyful melody

10. How did Elise's birth mother feel as she handed Elise over to Miriam?

A) Angry

B) Anxious

C) Exhausted but thankful

D) Reluctant

Seven

Scammed

True story

We were in Tirana, Albania when we received a request from a man named Jay for a six-week long Airbnb booking. As Airbnb hosts, this was a rare opportunity, and we were excited. It meant more income for our overseas travels. Jay spoke on the phone with Calvin and explained that his company was going to write us a check for his stay. He spoke to Calvin for half an hour talking about his twin daughters, travel, God, and coffee. We now think he had checked out our social media profiles to know just what to talk about. He was truly a professional scam artist. We didn't really see any red flags, so we said okay and let him into our Airbnb without any form of payment. This was our biggest mistake.

Days later after not receiving any form of payment, we became suspicious. Jay wasn't responding to our messages. We asked our neighbor Jan to check on the house, and she said no one was there. We had a sinking feeling in our stomachs. For some reason, Jay had closed all the curtains and taped a towel over the front door window. We had our locks changed immediately. Thankfully the house appeared untouched, but a month later, we noticed something strange. Checks were being forged in our name, and a credit card that I hadn't used in months had charges on it. We discovered Jay had broken into a locked closet and stolen a book of checks and a credit card. It turns out that his plan was to steal money from us. He had written checks for more than $4,000!

It was a long and messy process, but our bank and credit card company ended up reimbursing us all of our money. We had to file a report with the police and have calls with a detective all while overseas. Unfortunately our security camera wasn't working at the time, so we had no video footage of him. We learned our lesson the hard way this time. We never went outside of the Airbnb app for any bookings again. We didn't want to take the risk, and we learned that though most people are good, there are people out there looking to scam you.

◆◆◆◆◆◆◆◆◆◆◆◆◆◆◆◆◆◆◆◆◆◆◆◆◆◆◆◆◆◆◆◆◆◆

Word List

rare (**adjective**) - not common or usual; not often done, seen, or happening

income (**noun**) - money that is earned from work, investments, business, etc.

check (**noun**) - a paper form of money

twin (**noun**) - either one of two babies that are born at the same time to the same mother

scam artist (noun) - someone who attempts to trick people by deceitful behavior

red flag (noun) - a warning sign

suspicious (adjective) - cautious; showing distrust in someone

sinking feeling (noun) - a feeling of dread or discouragement

curtain (noun) - a piece of cloth that hangs down from above a window and can be used to cover the window

forge (verb) - to illegally sign someone else's name on a document

charge (noun) - a fee charged on a credit card

messy (adjective) - complicated

reimburse (verb) - to pay someone an amount of money equal to an amount that person has spent

file (verb) - to give (something, such as an official form or a legal document) to someone in authority so that it can be considered, dealt with, approved, etc.

report (noun) - a written or spoken description of a situation, event, etc.

detective (noun) - a person whose job is to find information about something or someone

footage (noun) - recorded video material

scam (verb) - to deceive someone, often in an attempt to get money

Multiple Choice Quiz

1. Where were the hosts when they received a request for a 6-week Airbnb booking?

A) Rome, Italy

B) Tirana, Albania

C) Paris, France

D) Barcelona, Spain

2. Why were the hosts excited about the Airbnb booking request?

A) It meant more income for travel.

B) They were fans of the guest's company.

C) The guest promised a good review.

D) The guest was a family member.

3. How did the guest convince the hosts to let him in without payment?

A) He threatened them.

B) He was a longtime friend.

C) He claimed his company would write them a check.

D) He offered to pay in cash.

4. What did the guest discuss with Calvin during their phone conversation?

A) Business

B) Travel

C) Cooking

D) Sports

5. Why did the hosts become suspicious days later?
A) The guest was not social.
B) They hadn't received any form of payment.
C) The guest left without notice.
D) The guest complained about the accommodation.

6. Who did the hosts ask to check on their house when the guest stopped responding?
A) Jan, the neighbor
B) The police
C) A security guard
D) Their relative

7. What did the hosts notice when they changed their locks?
A) The house was in disarray.
B) The curtains were closed.
C) The guest left a note.
D) The front door was missing.

8. How did the scam artist break into the hosts' closet?
A) Through a window
B) By picking the lock
C) By using a stolen key
D) The story doesn't mention how.

9. What was the total amount the scam artist wrote in forged checks?
A) $1,000
B) $2,500
C) $4,000
D) $6,000

10. What lesson did the hosts learn from this experience?
A) Always trust guests who talk about God.
B) Only accept cash payments.
C) Never go outside of the Airbnb app for bookings.
D) Security cameras are unnecessary for Airbnb hosts.

Eight

Root Canal

Tom's tooth had been hurting for over a week. He thought it was because of a popcorn kernel that got stuck back there, but then he realized that it wasn't that. The popcorn kernel was long gone, but Tom was still in excruciating pain. He couldn't focus on work or anything else. He made an emergency appointment with his dentist because Advil wasn't helping the pain.

After a set of x-rays, Tom's dentist confirmed that Tom would need a root canal. Unfortunately, his dental insurance didn't cover the $1,200 fee, but Tom's dentist's office told him they accepted monthly payments for up to a year. Tom had no other choice, so he agreed to it. Considering his high level of pain, the dentist said he could do the root canal on the spot. The dentist gave Tom some local anesthesia to numb the pain and then got to work. Tom chose to listen to music during the process to make it more durable. The dentist drilled a bit, but overall, it was a fairly quick procedure that lasted around 35 minutes. Tom's mouth was so numb that he didn't feel anything during the whole procedure.

"Good as new," his dentist proclaimed. The dentist told Tom that he would be numb for a couple of hours, but that he was okay to drink and eat. Tom decided to stop and get a milkshake on his way home, but he was so numb that he couldn't manage to drink through the straw. Ice cream from the milkshake was dribbling down his chin and into his lap. He laughed to himself as he imagined what a sight he must be.

Tom decided to take the rest of the afternoon off work. He settled onto his couch to catch up on some episodes of *The Walking Dead*. A few hours went by, and Tom was relieved that his tooth was no longer in pain. His dentist had warned him that he would most likely eventually need a crown but that he could probably put it off for a year or two. A crown was going to cost Tom an additional $1200.

"I think I should have become a dentist," Tom thought to himself. "I'm going to go broke with all these dental bills!"

◆◆◆◆◆◆◆◆◆◆◆◆◆◆◆◆◆◆◆◆◆◆◆◆◆◆◆◆◆◆◆◆◆

Word List

excruciating (**adjective**) - intensely painful

root canal (**noun**) - an expensive procedure to remove the infected pulp and nerve in the root of a tooth

monthly (**adverb**) - once a month

payment (**noun**) - an amount of money that is paid for something

on the spot (**idiom**) - at that exact moment

anesthesia (**noun**) - medicine used to numb an area of the body before a procedure

numb (**verb**) - to cause (a part of the body) to be unable to feel anything

drill (**verb**) - to make a hole in something with a drill

milkshake (**noun**) - a drink made with milk and ice cream

straw (**noun**) - a thin tube used for sucking up a drink

dribble (**verb**) - to fall or flow in small drops

catch up on (**phrasal verb**) - to learn the most recent information

crown (**noun**) - a tooth-shaped cap used to cover weak, broken, or decayed teeth

to go broke (**phrase**) - to spend or lose all of your money

◆◆◆◆◆◆◆◆◆◆◆◆◆◆◆◆◆◆◆◆◆◆◆◆◆◆◆◆◆◆

Multiple Choice Quiz

1. Why did Tom initially think his tooth was hurting?
A) He had a cavity.
B) He had a popcorn kernel stuck in his tooth.
C) He had a cracked tooth.
D) He had sensitive teeth.

2. What realization did Tom have about the cause of his tooth pain?

A) It was due to a cavity.

B) The popcorn kernel was still stuck.

C) It wasn't related to the popcorn kernel.

D) He needed braces.

3. Why did Tom make an emergency appointment with his dentist?

A) He wanted a routine check-up.

B) Advil didn't alleviate the pain.

C) He needed a teeth cleaning.

D) He wanted a second opinion.

4. What did the x-rays reveal about Tom's tooth condition?

A) He needed braces.

B) He had a popcorn kernel stuck.

C) He needed a root canal.

D) He had a cavity.

5. Did Tom's dental insurance cover the root canal fee?

A) Yes.

B) No.

C) The story didn't say.

D) It covered half of it.

6. How did Tom pay for the root canal procedure?

A) Cash

B) Credit card

C) Monthly payments

D) Dental insurance covered it.

7. What was Tom's experience during the root canal procedure?
A) Prolonged pain
B) Numbness due to anesthesia
C) Laughter and joy
D) Soreness and discomfort

8. What did Tom decide to do after the root canal procedure?
A) Go back to work
B) Get another dental opinion
C) Have a milkshake
D) Avoid eating or drinking

9. Why did Tom struggle to drink his milkshake?
A) He was too full.
B) The milkshake was too cold.
C) He was too numb.
D) The straw was broken.

10. What future dental procedure did Tom's dentist mention?
A) Teeth cleaning
B) Filling a cavity
C) Getting braces
D) Needing a crown

Nine

Speeding Ticket

Tessa's stomach sank as she saw the blue flashing lights and heard the siren behind her. "Cool, a police car," her eight year old piped up from the backseat.

"No, it's not cool. I was speeding. I don't want another speeding ticket. My car insurance will go up again," she responded.

The police officer asked to see Tessa's license and registration. Tessa knew the drill and already had them ready, so she handed them to him. He asked her if she knew that she was speeding, going 50 mph in a 35 mph zone. Tessa responded that she hadn't realized. She was only focused on picking up her daughter from her dance lesson.

Tessa pleaded with the police officer not to give her a ticket, saying that she would pay better attention when driving. He didn't seem too sympathetic and said that he would be right back. He walked to his car and then came back with a piece of paper. He said that he wrote down that she was only going ten miles over and that it would only be one point on her license so that it shouldn't be a big deal. Tessa swallowed her anger and took a deep breath. She vowed to go to court and fight the ticket.

"Mommy, do you have to go to jail?" her son asked.

"No, no, don't worry. Mommy just has to slow down when she's driving," Tessa answered. She was beyond annoyed, but she didn't want to put a damper on their outing, so she cheerfully smiled and turned on some pop music. "How about let's go get your sister and go pick up some pizza for dinner," she said to her son.

Her son pumped his first into the air and proclaimed that it was a great day. He had seen a police car with sirens, and he was going to eat his favorite food. It wasn't Tessa's favorite day, but pizza always made everything a little bit better.

Word List

stomach sinks (idiom) - you have a bad feeling

siren (noun) - a loud, high-pitched warning sound, often from a police car or firetruck

pipe up (phrasal verb) - to start talking

speeding ticket (noun) - a piece of paper that a police officer gives to someone who was driving too fast and that indicates a fine that the driver will have to pay

know the drill (idiom) - to know how something is done

registration (**noun**) - a document showing that something (such as a vehicle) has been officially registered

mph - abbreviation for miles per hour

plead (**verb**) - to beg

state (**verb**) - to say

point (**noun**) - When you get a speeding ticket, you get points on your license that count against you. If you get an accumulation of too many points, you can lose your license.

put a damper on (**idiom**) - to make (something) less strong, active, or exciting

◆◆◆◆◆◆◆◆◆◆◆◆◆◆◆◆◆◆◆◆◆◆◆◆◆◆◆◆◆◆◆◆

Multiple Choice Quiz

1. What was Tessa's initial reaction when she saw the police car behind her?
A) Excitement
B) Annoyance
C) Sadness
D) Indifference

2. What did Tessa's son think about the police car?

A) It was cool

B) He was scared

C) He was annoyed

D) He felt indifferent

3. Why was Tessa concerned about getting a ticket?

A) She had outstanding fines.

B) Her insurance would increase.

C) She didn't have a license.

D) She was on probation.

4. What reason did Tessa give for speeding when questioned by the police officer?

A) She didn't realize she was speeding.

B) She was in a hurry to get home.

C) She was testing her car's speed.

D) She was racing another driver.

5. How did Tessa react when the police officer mentioned writing a ticket?

A) She laughed.

B) She pleaded with him.

C) She didn't respond.

D) She argued aggressively.

6. What did the police officer write on the piece of paper?

A) Tessa's home address

B) A warning for speeding

C) She was only going ten miles over.

D) Directions to the police station

7. How did Tessa feel about the police officer's decision?

A) Relieved

B) Angry

C) Indifferent

D) Excited

8. What did Tessa vow to do after receiving the ticket?

A) Pay it immediately

B) Go to court and fight it

C) Ignore it

D) Apologize to the police officer

9. How did Tessa reassure her son when he asked if she had to go to jail?

A) She told him not to worry.

B) She said she might go to jail.

C) She didn't respond.

D) She promised to take him to jail with her.

10. What made Tessa's son proclaim it was a great day in the end?

A) Picking up his sister from dance class

B) Going to jail

C) Eating pizza

D) Winning a prize

GET THE FREE AUDIO!
SCAN THIS QR CODE

GET THE AUDIOBOOK

https://bit.ly/amazon-advanced-short-story-audio
Any issues? audio@learnenglishwithcamille.com

Ten

Rollerblading Mishaps

TRUE STORY

As kids, my sisters and I loved to rollerblade in our driveway. We rarely wore helmets or knee pads, and we would cruise around for hours, our hair whipping behind us. One afternoon, we were out blading and having the time of our lives. I thought my younger sister Kimberly was chasing me, but it turns out, she wasn't. But thinking she was, I took off as fast as I could, and I tripped; I put both arms out to break my fall. That didn't go so well. I landed so hard on my arm that it literally snapped in two. I was in so much pain. I remember my parents telling me to get in the car. To this day, I don't know if I was in shock or what, but I never cried.

The doctor confirmed that I had broken both bones in my forearm and that I would need a cast going up past my elbow. He said that he could put my arm in place without putting me under because I was strong. The rest was a blur. Luckily it was my left arm rather than my right because I am right-handed.

I remember my mother having to help me in the shower. I wasn't allowed to get my cast wet, so we would cover it with a plastic bag. Wearing the cast was itchy, and after a few weeks, it started to smell pretty bad. I had to go in for regular check-ups, but the doctor assured us that everything was healing just fine. My friends signed my cast and thought it was cool. The cast had to be on for what felt like forever, but in reality, it was six weeks.

Eventually the cast came off. Unfortunately for me, the following year I fell hard on my wrist while playing basketball and fractured it. It wasn't an obvious fracture, but my wrist was in a lot of pain, so my mom took me to the doctor. Another cast went on, this time the other arm. Don't worry, though. It was the last time I broke anything.

Word List

rollerblade (verb) - to move or glide quickly along a surface with boots that have wheels

helmet (noun) - a hard hat that is worn to protect your head

cruise around (phrasal verb) - to move or drive around

whip (verb) - to flow from side to side

blade (verb) - (slang) to skate using rollerblades

trip (verb) - to fall or almost fall

break my fall (idiom) - to catch myself while falling

snap (verb) - to break

cast (noun) - a hard bandage to protect bones while they are healing

in place (phrase) - in its usual or correct position

put under (phrasal verb) - to sedate

blur (noun) - something that is difficult to remember

right-handed (adjective) - using the right hand more easily than the left hand

itchy (adjective) - feeling or having an itch- something you need to scratch

wrist (noun) - the part of the arm where the hand and lower arm meet

fracture (noun) - a break in the bone

◆◆◆◆◆◆◆◆◆◆◆◆◆◆◆◆◆◆◆◆◆◆◆◆◆◆◆◆◆◆◆◆

Multiple Choice Quiz

1. What did Camille and her sisters enjoy doing as kids?
A) Playing video games
B) Riding bikes
C) Rollerblading
D) Skateboarding

2. What safety gear did Camille and her sisters rarely wear while rollerblading?

A) Helmets and knee pads

B) Elbow pads and gloves

C) Shin guards and wrist guards

D) Protective vests and ankle guards

3. What led to Camille's injury while rollerblading?

A) Trying to get away from her sister

B) Attempting a trick

C) Racing with friends

D) Riding too slowly

4. How did Camille react to the pain of her broken arm?

A) She cried loudly.

B) She didn't cry at all.

C) She screamed for help.

D) She called for her parents.

5. Why did the doctor say he could put Camille's arm in place without anesthesia?

A) Camille was too scared.

B) He thought Camille was strong.

C) Anesthesia was not available.

D) It was a quick procedure.

6. What was the duration of time Camille had to wear the cast on her left arm?
A) 2 weeks
B) 4 weeks
C) 6 weeks
D) 8 weeks

7. How did Camille protect her cast while showering?
A) She didn't shower for six weeks.
B) She used a waterproof cast.
C) She covered it with a plastic bag.
D) She removed the cast for showers.

8. What did Camille injure the following year while playing basketball?
A) Left wrist
B) Right wrist
C) Both arms
D) Right elbow

9. How did Camille's friends react to her cast?
A) They thought it was boring.
B) They didn't notice it.
C) They signed it and thought it was cool.
D) They made fun of her.

10. What assurance did the doctor give Camille during the regular check-ups?
A) Camille needed surgery.
B) Everything was healing well.
C) The cast needed to stay on longer.
D) Camille would never heal completely.

Eleven

Beginning College

Katie was so excited, but at the same time, she was so nervous to go to college. She was going to be living in the campus dorms, and she only knew two girls from her high school that were also going there. They had different majors, so the likelihood of running into them was small. Katie had already had freshmen orientation and saw that she was sharing a room with a girl named Sharon Stone. Katie had enrolled in five classes: algebra, English, science, sociology, and writing. Between her classes and volleyball, she knew she wouldn't have much free time.

She had gotten a full ride because of volleyball. If it wasn't for her scholarship, she most likely would have had to take out loans for school. College was expensive these days, and her parents weren't made of money, but they had been so generous to buy her a new laptop and some new clothes. Katie was only thirty minutes away from her parents' house, so she could still go home on weekends to do her laundry when she ran out of clean clothes. She had had to give up her job working as a barista because she knew her classes and volleyball would take up most of her time.

Katie was only moving with two suitcases. She didn't want her dorm room to be cluttered. She had read a study that said less clutter equals more focus. She had just finished zipping up her backpack when she heard her dad calling her name.

"Are you ready?" he hollered up the stairs.

Katie took one last look at her room and sighed. It was the good kind of sigh, the end of an era kind of sigh. She was lugging her suitcases down the hall when she bumped into her dad. He offered to help her and grabbed both the suitcases.

Her parents were going to drive her to school and drop her off. She wouldn't have a car, so she was going to take the bus home on the weekends. Katie didn't want the extra hassle and expense of owning a car. Katie's mom was already waiting for them in the car. She was teary eyed because Katie was her first child to go off to college, and it just wouldn't be the same anymore. Her little baby was growing up. Katie's dad popped the bags in the trunk, and they took off down the road.

Word List

college (noun)- a school that offers courses leading to a degree (such as a bachelor's degree or an associate's degree)

dorm (noun) - an informal word for dormitory— a building on a school campus that has rooms where students can live

likelihood (**noun**) - the chance that something will happen

freshmen orientation (**noun**) - a period of time before the semester begins when new students can start to become familiar with a college

volleyball (**noun**) - a game in which two teams of players hit a ball back and forth over a high net

full ride (**idiom**) - an offer by a college or university to pay all costs for the studies of a person

scholarship (**noun**) - an amount of money that is given by a school, an organization, etc., to a student to help pay for the student's education

loan (**noun**) - an amount of money that is given to someone for a period of time with a promise that it will be paid back; an amount of money that is borrowed

made of money (**idiom**) - rich; wealthy

barista (**noun**) - someone who works in a coffee shop and makes drinks for people

take up (**phrasal verb**) - to fill; to occupy

cluttered (**adjective**) - untidy; filled with too many things

holler (**verb**) - to yell

end of an era (**phrase**) - the end of a significant period of life

lug (**verb**) - to haul

bump into (phrasal verb) - to meet (someone) by chance

pop (verb) - to put

◆◆◆◆◆◆◆◆◆◆◆◆◆◆◆◆◆◆◆◆◆◆◆◆◆◆◆◆◆◆◆◆◆◆◆

Multiple Choice Quiz

1. Where was Katie going to be living?
A) The college dorms
B) Off-campus housing
C) At home
D) Her own apartment

2. Who was Katie's roommate in the dorm going to be?
A) Sharon Stone
B) Katie Stone
C) Unknown
D) Two girls from high school

3. How many classes did Katie enroll in for her first semester?
A) 3
B) 4
C) 5
D) 6

4. Why did Katie receive a full-ride scholarship?

A) Excellent grades

B) Athletic achievement in volleyball

C) Outstanding performance in writing

D) Financial need

5. Why did Katie decide to give up her job as a barista?

A) She wanted to focus on her studies and volleyball.

B) She found a better-paying job.

C) She didn't enjoy being a barista.

D) She had a falling out with her coworkers.

6. How far away is Katie's college from her parents' house?

A) 15 minutes

B) 30 minutes

C) 1 hour

D) 2 hours

7. What did Katie's parents generously buy her for college?

A) A new car

B) A new phone

C) A new laptop and clothes

D) A dorm room decoration

8. How many suitcases was Katie going to bring to college?

A) 1

B) 2

C) 3

D) 4

9. What was Katie's reason for not bringing a car to college?
A) She couldn't afford it.
B) Campus parking was expensive.
C) She preferred taking the bus.
D) It was too much hassle and too expensive.

10. Who was going to drive Katie to college?
A) Her parents
B) Her dad
C) Her brother
D) Her best friend

Twelve

Restored Hope

True story

We have a house in America that we live in when we're there. I say "when we're there" because we travel a lot. Our garage is connected to our house; we converted it to a suite, which we rent out to guests. Guests who stay in the suite always have access to our pool. One hot summer afternoon, we happened to be in the pool; South Carolina summers can be brutal, and having a pool is a delightful treat.

Our kids practically live in the pool in the summer. You would think we would bump into our guests all the time, but we actually don't. It's a rare occurrence that our guests are using the pool at the same time as us. I am always curious about who people are, so when we end up sharing the pool, I start chatting and asking them questions. Our guest Daniel happened to be from the Dominican Republic but was living in the US. Daniel was developing his photography skills and asked if he could take some photos of my kids and me in the pool. He then later edited them and sent them to me. They were pretty great.

Daniel was a big guy with dark skin. I treated him with kindness but nothing out of the ordinary. I had a pleasant time chatting with him and his girlfriend. He got a bit emotional and made a statement that shocked me. "You've restored my hope in humanity," he said.

I thought it was a pretty profound statement to make. Unfortunately, it turns out that he had been treated pretty badly by some Americans. He expressed some sadness when he talked about the negative encounters he had had with some Americans. Sadly, racism still exists, and he was feeling the effects. I was saddened to hear this but thankful that I had given him some hope once again. It reminded me that kindness always wins. We don't know what people are going through or what they have gone through, but everyone deserves to be treated with respect and kindness, no matter what they look like or where they are from.

Word List

rent out (phrasal verb) - to allow someone to stay somewhere in return for payment

brutal (adjective) - very bad or unpleasant

treat (noun) - something special or pleasant

treat (verb) - to act toward someone in a certain way

pleasant (adjective) - enjoyable

emotional (**adjective**) - expressing or having strong feelings, such as sadness or joy

restore (**verb**) - to bring (something) back into existence

profound (**adjective**) - meaningful; significant

racism (**noun**) - poor treatment of or violence against people because of their skin color

◆◆◆◆◆◆◆◆◆◆◆◆◆◆◆◆◆◆◆◆◆◆◆◆◆◆◆◆◆◆◆◆

Multiple Choice Quiz

1. Where is the house in the story located?
A) France
B) Dominican Republic
C) South Carolina
D) California

2. What is a unique feature of the house?
A) Rooftop terrace
B) Indoor garden
C) Pool shared with guests
D) Private beach

3. What prompted Daniel to take photos of Camille's family in the pool?

A) He was a professional photographer.

B) He wanted to practice his photography skills.

C) Camille asked him to.

D) It was part of the rental agreement.

4. What was Daniel's nationality?

A) American

B) French

C) Dominican

D) Spanish

5. How did the author describe Daniel's physical appearance?

A) Thin with fair skin

B) Big with dark skin

C) Muscular with blonde hair

D) Tall with red hair

6. What did Daniel say that surprised Camille?

A) He was moving back to the Dominican Republic.

B) He was a professional photographer.

C) Camille had restored his hope in humanity.

D) He wanted to buy Camille's house.

7. What skill was Daniel working on improving?

A) Cooking

B) Swimming

C) Photography

D) Gardening

8. What emotion did Daniel express during the encounter at the pool?
A) Happiness
B) Sadness
C) Anger
D) Excitement

9. What did Camille learn from her encounter with Daniel?
A) Photography skills
B) How Daniel had been treated poorly
C) Swimming techniques
D) Gardening tips

10. What did Camille emphasize as the key takeaway from the experience?
A) Racism is unavoidable.
B) Kindness always wins.
C) Americans are unfriendly.
D) Photography is a powerful art form.

Thirteen

Rollerblading in Barcelona

TRUE STORY

We had been traveling for almost eight months when we arrived in Barcelona, so we were feeling a bit burned out. Barcelona has some of the BEST rollerblading paths in all of Europe, so Calvin took the kids out and bought them rollerblades, helmets, knee pads, elbow pads, and wrist pads. We were traveling with only two suitcases at the time, so this extra gear was definitely not going to fit in our luggage. Calvin said he wanted to settle down; he was buying everything as a way to say that we would be settling down. We toyed with the idea of settling in Spain because we truly adored the country, and we had lived there for two years in the past.

Back to blading...the kids learned so quickly. I was so nervous because I had broken my arm rollerblading when I was younger. Maddox, our oldest son, was already doing jumps and spins by the end of week one. Ivory learned a little more slowly but not by much. She worked hard to keep up with her older brother. We were impressed.

We were staying in our friend's apartment with a tiny elevator, and every time the kids wanted to go rollerblading (which was every day), we had to cram into the elevator with all their clunky blades and gear. The blades and gear were so heavy and awkward, but the kids didn't mind. A few times, we rode buses to go to specific paths for them to blade, but most of the time we just went to one of the parks outside our door. The kids fell countless times, but they loved it, and thankfully they never got seriously hurt.

We ended up buying another suitcase for the rollerblades and gear and took it all to Portugal, which is where we are currently living. The kids continue to use their blades every week. I'm thankful we decided to stay in Portugal for a while because it's not super practical to travel the world with rollerblades, and we needed a place to settle down after feeling so burned out.

Word List

burned out (adjective) - very tired; no desire to continue what you are doing

wrist pad (noun) - a pad worn to protect your wrist

gear (noun) - equipment such as pads and helmets

settle down (phrasal verb) - to stay in one place for an extended period of time

toy with (phrasal verb) - to consider; to think about something

elevator (noun) - a machine used for carrying people and things to different levels in a building

clunky (adjective) - heavy; large and awkward

Multiple Choice Quiz

1. What prompted Calvin to buy rollerblades and gear for the kids in Barcelona?
A) They were starting a rollerblading club.
B) Calvin wanted to encourage them to stay active.
C) Calvin wanted to settle down.
D) Rollerblading was a popular sport in Barcelona.

2. Why did the family consider settling in Spain?
A) They loved the rollerblading paths.
B) They had friends there.
C) They found a great apartment.
D) They adored the country.

3. How did the kids adapt to rollerblading?
A) They were hesitant.
B) They learned quickly.
C) They didn't like it.
D) They refused to try.

4. What skill did Maddox, the oldest son, learn by the end of week one?
A) Backflips
B) Jumps and spins
C) Skating backward
D) Figure skating moves

5. Why did the family have to pack into a tiny elevator every time the kids wanted to go rollerblading?
A) The elevator was the only way to reach the rollerblading paths.
B) It was a fun family tradition.
C) The apartment had strict rules.
D) The rollerblades were heavy and awkward.

6. How did the kids travel to specific rollerblading paths on some occasions?
A) Rollerblading
B) Bicycles
C) Buses
D) Taxis

7. Where did the family end up taking the rollerblades and gear after Barcelona?
A) Back to the United States
B) Portugal
C) Spain
D) France

8. Why did the family decide to stay in Portugal for a while?
A) They were burned out from traveling.
B) They found a great job opportunity.
C) Rollerblading paths were better in Portugal.
D) The kids wanted to attend school there.

9. How often do the kids continue to use their rollerblades in Portugal?
A) Every day
B) Every week
C) Rarely
D) Only on weekends

10. What does Camille express gratitude for in the end?
A) Having friends in Barcelona
B) The decision to settle down
C) Buying another suitcase
D) Staying in Portugal

Fourteen

A Surprise Guest

Jude and Violet were cleaning up the kitchen after enjoying some scrumptious salmon with asparagus. They didn't have any plans, but they were hoping to turn in early; Jude had a deadline at work, so he had been going to bed early every day that week. He was so tired and thankful that tomorrow was Friday. Violet was pregnant with their first child. She was in her first trimester, and she was exhausted. She couldn't stay up past 9:30 pm.

Their doorbell rang, and Jude said he would get it. He figured it was his neighbor stopping by to chat. He opened the door and was greeted by a HUGE surprise and a familiar face. "How did you, what did you..." Jude said, at a complete loss for words.

It was his best friend Damien from high school, who Jude hadn't seen in two years. Damien had been living in Paris because of a job transfer. Jude gave Damien the biggest hug and invited him inside. They had just chatted last week on the phone, but Damien hadn't mentioned visiting or anything about coming back to the US.

"What are you doing here?!" Jude exclaimed.

Damien explained that his two-year work contract was over and that his company was paying him even more money to transfer back to Chicago. "I thought it would be fun to surprise you," he said, grinning.

At that moment, Violet entered the room, gave Damien a big hug, and offered him some food. Damien politely declined the food saying he had just eaten but took her up on some coffee. They moved into the living room, where they chatted for the next several hours non-stop. Violet excused herself at 9:25 to go to sleep, but Damien and Jude just kept chatting, making plans to go hiking and out to dinner the following week. Jude was beyond stoked to have his bestie back in town.

❖❖❖❖❖❖❖❖❖❖❖❖❖❖❖❖❖❖❖❖❖❖❖❖❖❖❖❖❖❖❖❖

Word List

scrumptious (adjective) - very delicious

asparagus (noun) - a long and thin green vegetable

turn in (phrasal verb) - go to bed

deadline (noun) - the latest time by which something should be completed

first trimester (noun) - the first three months of pregnancy

neighbor (noun) - the person who lives next door to you

at a loss for words (idiom) - speechless; unable to think of anything to say

politely (adverb) - nicely

stoked (adjective) - extremely happy

bestie (noun) - best friend

◆◆◆◆◆◆◆◆◆◆◆◆◆◆◆◆◆◆◆◆◆◆◆◆◆◆◆◆◆

Multiple Choice Quiz

1. Why was Jude hoping to turn in early that night?
A) He had plans the next day.
B) He was tired from work.
C) Violet was not feeling well.
D) They had a party to attend.

2. What had Jude and Violet just finished eating before the doorbell rang?
A) Pizza
B) Salmon with asparagus
C) Spaghetti
D) Grilled chicken

3. Why had Jude been going to work early every day that week?
A) He had a deadline to meet.
B) He had a morning meeting.
C) He enjoyed the early morning hours.
D) His boss asked him to.

4. Why was Violet usually in bed by 9:30 pm?

A) She had a night job.

B) She had a strict bedtime routine.

C) She was pregnant and tired.

D) She had early morning plans.

5. Who did Jude think was at the door when the doorbell rang?

A) A salesperson

B) Violet's friend

C) His neighbor

D) A delivery person

6. Where had Damien been living for the past two years?

A) Paris

B) Chicago

C) New York

D) London

7. Why did Damien decide to surprise Jude and Violet?

A) He liked surprises.

B) It was Jude's birthday.

C) He thought it would be fun.

D) He didn't have anything else to do.

8. What did Damien's company do to convince him to transfer back to Chicago?

A) Gave him a promotion

B) Offered more vacation days

C) Increased his salary

D) Provided a better work schedule

9. How did Violet react when she first saw Damien?
A) She was shocked.
B) She gave him a big hug.
C) She offered him food.
D) She went to bed.

10. What plans did Jude and Damien make for the next week?
A) Movie night
B) Hiking and dinner
C) Shopping spree
D) Bowling tournament

Fifteen

Bitten by a Weever Fish

True story

We were at the beach in Dikili, Türkiye with one of our Turkish friends. It was extremely windy, but the water was warm, so the kids were swimming close to the shore. They love the water and never miss an opportunity to swim. Suddenly, we were startled by Maddox, our nine year old, screaming that he got bitten and that his foot hurt. We couldn't see anything, but his scream was so loud, and he wouldn't stop crying.

Inexperienced with the sea and assuming it may be a jellyfish sting, we figured he needed a doctor because we were uncertain how we could help him. Our friend Furkan located the nearest ER, which happened to be a minute from our house but 15 minutes from where we were.

Maddox screamed the whole time in the car saying, "I'll do anything for this pain to stop. This is the worst pain in my life."

We had never had to take our kids to the ER before. Calvin was a bit frazzled driving, definitely speeding as he tried to get to the ER as quickly as possible. We were googling cures online, but we still didn't know what had caused the pain. We read that soaking his foot in white vinegar with water would help, so we made a quick stop at a market to pick up the ingredients, but that didn't seem to help at all.

We showed up at the ER carrying Maddox in. Ivory was so shaken up that she threw up outside the ER. After taking one look, the doctors immediately knew it was from a weever fish and gave Maddox some local anesthesia. They ended up giving him two shots to help with the pain, saying that the pain from the venom can be a ten out of ten for the first two hours. They said there was nothing to remove and nothing we could do but wait. We waited at the ER for an hour, and then they released us to go home. Before we left, the doctor encouraged us to buy a special cream and ibuprofen. The cream would prevent infections, and the ibuprofen would keep the pain under control. We only paid $35 USD for the visit.

By the time we got home, Maddox was feeling much better. The pain had subsided. Needless to say, he was a bit traumatized by the experience. We were too! It's hard to see your child in such agony. Furkan felt so bad too, but we were very thankful he was there with us. We bought ALL our kids water shoes after that experience and we had to reassure our kids that it was a freak accident and that it most likely wouldn't happen again. Luckily, they ended up back in the water again… with their water shoes on.

Word List

ER (noun) - abbreviation for emergency room

shore (noun) - the land along the edge of an area of water (such as an ocean, lake, etc.)

startle (verb) - to surprise or frighten (someone) suddenly

jellyfish (noun) - a jelly-like creature in the sea that can sting

frazzled (adjective) - nervous; upset

speed (verb) - to drive faster than the speed limit

cure (noun) - something that ends a problem or improves a bad situation

soak (verb) - to cover in liquid

shaken up (adjective) - shocked; upset

throw up (phrasal verb) - to vomit

weever fish (noun) - a slender fish that releases venom

venom (noun) - poison that is produced by an animal and used to kill or injure, usually through biting or stinging

USD - abbreviation for the United States Dollar

subside (verb) - to become less intense

traumatized (adjective) - affected by physical or emotional pain

agony (**noun**) - extreme pain

water shoes (**noun**) - a special shoe to protect the foot while in water

freak accident (**noun**) - an incident that occurs under highly unusual and unlikely circumstances

◆◆◆◆◆◆◆◆◆◆◆◆◆◆◆◆◆◆◆◆◆◆◆◆◆◆◆◆◆◆

Multiple Choice Quiz

1. Where was the family when Maddox got bitten?
A) In a market
B) In a car
C) At a beach in Türkiye
D) At the ER

2. Why did Maddox go to the ER?
A) He got a jellyfish sting.
B) He got bitten by a weever fish.
C) He had a fever.
D) He needed stitches.

3. How far was the ER from the beach?
A) 1 minute
B) 10 minutes
C) 15 minutes
D) 30 minutes

4. What did Maddox say about the pain during the car ride to the ER?

A) It was manageable.

B) It was the worst pain of his life.

C) It didn't hurt.

D) It was slightly painful.

5. What did they initially think caused Maddox's pain?

A) A jellyfish sting

B) Sunburn

C) A weever fish bite

D) A sea urchin encounter

6. What remedy did they try before going to the ER?

A) Antibiotics

B) Painkillers

C) A white vinegar soak

D) An ice pack

7. How did Ivory react to the situation?

A) She was calm.

B) She threw up.

C) She swam to the shore.

D) She took charge of the situation.

8. How much did they pay for the ER visit?

A) $10 USD

B) $20 USD

C) $35 USD

D) It was free.

9. What did the doctors say about the pain from the weever fish bite?

A) It lasts for a few minutes.

B) It can be a 10 out of 10 for the first 2 hours.

C) It's not painful at all.

D) It gets worse over time.

10. What precautionary measures did they take after the incident?

A) Applied sunscreen

B) Avoided the beach

C) Bought water shoes

D) Used insect repellent

Sixteen

The Coolest Babysitter

The Cooper kids loved their babysitter Mandy. She came up with the most creative and fun ideas. Last week, she built an epic fort out of old sheets. The Cooper kids were a bit of a wild tribe: Axel was three, Andy was six, and Asher was seven. Mandy grew up with all brothers, so it was like she was at home. She babysat for the Coopers every Wednesday and Friday from 10:00 am-3:00 pm. The Coopers paid her $10 an hour; she was saving up for college, so she was happy to have a job. She wanted to study psychology, and she hoped to one day become a school counselor. She loved kids, and she felt drawn to them.

The Cooper's gave her free rein of their kitchen, and this week she was planning on making gingerbread cutout cookies with the kids. It was December, and everyone was in the Christmas spirit. Christmas music was blasting on the TV when she walked in the door, and the boys were jumping on the couches. They came running to her with the gingerbread cutouts. They knew they were going to bake cookies today, and they were so excited. Mrs. Cooper said a quick hello but then rushed out the door for a work meeting. She was a book publisher at one of the biggest publishing firms in the country. Mr. Cooper was already at work. He left every morning at 7:30 am.

Mandy was excited to start baking with the boys. They helped her measure the ingredients and put them into the bowl. Axel dropped an egg on the floor, and then Andy slipped on the egg. He didn't get hurt, but Mandy had to throw his clothes in the wash. After that, everything went pretty smoothly. Mandy rolled out the dough, and the boys had fun making gingerbread cookies of all sizes. After baking them in the oven and letting them cool, they decorated them with vanilla icing.

The boys wanted to bring some cookies to their next door neighbors, so Mandy put a few on a plate and wrote a note that said "Merry Christmas." Asher put on his coat and boots and took the cookies over. Soon, the snow began to fall. The kids wanted to go out and play, so Mandy helped bundle them up in their snowsuits and boots. They spent the rest of the afternoon building snowmen and a snow fort. They couldn't wait for Mandy to come back again.

Word List

babysitter (**noun**) - a person who is paid to take care of children

epic (**adjective**) - incredible

fort (**noun**) - a play area for kids, usually covered

tribe (**noun**) - group of people

free rein (idiom) - the freedom to do, say, or feel what you want

cutout cookies (noun) - a type of cookie where you cut the dough into shapes

blast (verb) - to play very loudly

rush (verb) - to leave in a hurry

slip (verb) - to fall

dough (noun) - a mixture of flour, water, and other ingredients that is baked to make bread, cookies, etc

icing (noun) - frosting

bundle up (phrasal verb) - to put on a lot of warm clothes

snowman (noun) - a representation of a human figure created with snow

Multiple Choice Quiz

1. How many children does the Cooper family have?
A) 1
B) 2
C) 3
D) 4

2. What is Mandy's ambition for her future career?

A) Chef

B) School counselor

C) Book publisher

D) Psychologist

3. How often does Mandy babysit for the Coopers?

A) Once a week

B) Twice a week

C) Every day

D) Only on weekends

4. How much do the Coopers pay Mandy per hour?

A) $5

B) $8

C) $10

D) $15

5. What were the boys doing when Mandy walked in for babysitting?

A) They were sleeping.

B) They were playing video games.

C) They were jumping on the couches.

D) They were watching TV.

6. What did Axel do that caused a small mishap in the kitchen?

A) Spilled milk

B) Broke a plate

C) Dropped an egg

D) Ate cookie dough

7. What was Mandy planning to make with the kids this week?

A) Pizza

B) Gingerbread cutout cookies

C) Pancakes

D) Brownies

8. Where did Mrs. Cooper go during Mandy's babysitting time?

A) Grocery shopping

B) A work meeting

C) College

D) The gym

9. How did the boys deliver cookies to their neighbors?

A) By mail

B) By throwing them

C) By carrying them

D) By using a drone

10. What did the kids do after decorating the gingerbread cookies?

A) Played video games

B) Watched TV

C) Built snowmen and a snow fort

D) Took a nap

Seventeen

Our BEST day in Italy

True story

Italy is beautiful all year round, but visiting Italy in the off-season is cheaper. We were there in February, and it was quite cold. We were in Tuscany, and after searching online, Calvin found some free natural hot springs not too far from us. The kids were always down to go in the water, no matter the weather. It was three degrees Celsius (37 degrees Fahrenheit), the coldest day yet. There wasn't any snow, but the air was bitter cold. We drove our rental car for 40 minutes and then walked down a dirt road for another five minutes before we arrived at the hot springs. We saw one person that was just leaving.

The hot springs were awe-inspiring and so perfect for the day we were facing. We spent a good two hours soaking in the hot springs with a castle view. How amazing, right?! We were the only people there for an hour, and then a few people started to arrive.

They asked us to not share their "secret" springs on social media. "We don't want our springs to become popular," they told us.

We could see why they didn't want us posting anything online. We promised we wouldn't, and we spent the next hour chatting and getting to know them. The kids were like fish and didn't want to leave the springs. When it was time to finally leave, we had to take off our swimsuits and put our clothes back on. It was so cold that our youngest was almost crying, but we got dressed as quickly as possible and raced back to the car where we could turn the heat on.

We stopped at a local Tuscan restaurant that had amazing Google reviews. It didn't disappoint us. We had amazing Italian pasta, minestrone soup, and bread. I'm not much of a wine drinker, but Calvin tried the local red wine and really enjoyed it. This was a day to write home about. We love a good meal and a fun family outing. Our plan is to go back to Tuscany, but maybe this time we'll wait until March or April when the weather warms up.

Word List

off-season (noun) - not in the popular tourist season

down (adjective) - excited to participate in an activity

bitter (adjective) - extremely cold

awe-inspiring (adjective) - causes strong feelings of wonder

race (verb) - to go as quickly as possible

disappoint (**verb**) - to make (someone) unhappy by not being as good as expected or by not doing something that was hoped for or expected; to let down

something to write home about (**idiom**) - something exceptional or noteworthy; extra special

outing (**noun**) - a brief trip that people take for fun usually as a group

◆◆◆◆◆◆◆◆◆◆◆◆◆◆◆◆◆◆◆◆◆◆◆◆◆◆◆◆◆◆

Multiple Choice Quiz

1. Why did the family choose to visit Italy in February?
A) It's the warmest month.
B) It's the coldest month.
C) It's the cheapest month.
D) It's the most crowded month.

2. How did Calvin find the natural hot water springs?
A) Asked locals
B) Found a brochure
C) Searched online
D) Looked in a travel guidebook

3. What was the temperature on the day they visited the hot springs?
A) 10 degrees Celsius
B) 20 degrees Fahrenheit
C) 37 degrees Fahrenheit
D) 100 degrees Celsius

4. How did the family get to the hot springs?
A) Walked
B) Drove a rental car
C) Took a taxi
D) Rode bicycles

5. What did the family promise to the people they met at the hot springs?
A) To share the location on social media
B) To keep the springs a secret
C) To invite more people next time
D) To organize a public event

6. What did the family enjoy at the local Tuscan restaurant?
A) Pizza
B) Burgers
C) Italian pasta, minestrone soup, and bread
D) Mexican tacos

7. Why did the family hurry back to the car after leaving the hot springs?
A) To get home quickly
B) To avoid traffic
C) To turn on the heat and warm up
D) To catch a sunset

8. What drink did Calvin try at the local Tuscan restaurant?
A) Sparkling water
B) Italian soda
C) Espresso
D) Wine

9. What did the family do at the hot springs for about two hours?
A) Sunbathe
B) Read books
C) Soak in the springs
D) Hike in the mountains

10. When is the family considering returning to Tuscany
A) In February
B) In March or April
C) In the summer
D) In the fall

Eighteen

A Day at Sea

Zoey and Devon were so excited to go snorkeling in the Mexican Riviera. They had paid for a day boat cruise that included lunch and three hours on one of the world's best snorkeling reefs. They were nervous about the weather because the previous two days had been stormy. But the waters seemed calm and the clouds were breaking away, and the glorious sun was starting to shine. There was a family with two boys on the cruise. There were also three other couples. The boat ride was only 20 minutes, and by the time they reached the reef, the sun was shining brightly.

Zoey and Devon slathered on some SPF 30 sunblock and grabbed the fins and snorkels that were set out for them. They dove off the boat and couldn't believe the magic of the underwater world. They saw squids and turtles and many colorful varieties of fish. They even saw an octopus and three stingrays. The water was lukewarm and crystal clear. The experience was absolutely exhilarating and one of the best underwater moments of their lives.

"Mom, look, dolphins," one of the boys pointed out.

Sure enough, there were dolphins gliding effortlessly in the water just meters away from them. Zoey couldn't believe their luck. It was like they were in a movie or something.

For lunch, they ate grilled fish and french fries. It really hit the spot after being in the water for a couple of hours. After lunch, the captain of the boat took them to another spot of the reef 20 minutes away. It was just as beautiful as the first spot, and they got to spend another hour snorkeling and enjoying the water before it was time to pack up and go home.

Just when they were about to leave, Devon spotted a shiny object on the bottom of the ocean floor. He dove down and grabbed it. It was someone's old class ring from 1984. It was rusty, but there was a legible name carved on the inside next to the date. He decided he would google the name and try to find the owner. He knew the owner would be stunned as well, never expecting to get his class ring back after all these years.

❖❖❖❖❖❖❖❖❖❖❖❖❖❖❖❖❖❖❖❖❖❖❖❖❖❖❖❖❖❖

Word List

snorkel (verb) - to swim underwater near the ocean's surface while using a snorkel to breath

stormy (adjective) - rainy weather often accompanied by thunder and lightning

glorious (adjective) - beautiful

reef (noun) - a ridge of jagged rock, coral, or sand just above the surface of the sea

slather (verb) - to cover (something) with a thick layer of a liquid, cream, etc.

lukewarm (adjective) - not too hot or too cold

exhilarating (adjective) - very exciting; thrilling

glide (verb) - to move effortlessly and smoothly

hit the spot (idiom) - to be exactly what is needed

legible (adjective) - clear enough to be read

stunned (adjective) - surprised

◆◆◆◆◆◆◆◆◆◆◆◆◆◆◆◆◆◆◆◆◆◆◆◆◆◆◆◆◆◆◆◆

Multiple Choice Quiz

1. What were Zoey and Devon excited to do in the Mexican Riviera?
A) Go parasailing
B) Go scuba diving
C) Go snorkeling
D) Go jet skiing

2. What was a concern for Zoey and Devon before their snorkeling trip?
A) Food availability
B) Stormy weather
C) Boat engine trouble
D) Sunburn

3. How long was the boat ride to the snorkeling reef?
A) 5 minutes
B) 20 minutes
C) 1 hour
D) 3 hours

4. What did Zoey and Devon see during their snorkeling adventure?
A) Polar bears
B) Squids, turtles, colorful fish, octopuses, and stingrays
C) Penguins and sharks
D) Seagulls and seals

5. What did the family on the cruise spot in the water?
A) Mermaids
B) Dolphins
C) Whales
D) Sharks

6. What was served for lunch during the cruise?
A) Pizza
B) Grilled fish and french fries
C) Burgers and hot dogs
D) Sushi

7. How did Zoey and Devon feel about their underwater experience?

A) Disappointed

B) Bored

C) Exhilarated

D) Sleepy

8. What did Devon find on the ocean floor?

A) A seashell

B) A treasure chest

C) An old class ring

D) A pearl necklace

9. What did Devon decide to do with the class ring?

A) Keep it as a souvenir

B) Sell it

C) Throw it back in the ocean

D) Try to find its owner

10. What was the condition of the class ring Devon found?

A) Brand new

B) Shiny and polished

C) Rusty but with a legible name

D) Covered in diamonds

Nineteen

The Bet

True story

I was only sixteen years old when I started to work as a server for an amazing Chinese restaurant in my city. One day, the thirty-year-old Chinese owner, who also happened to be my boss, proposed a bet to me.

"I bet you $2,000 that you can't go two months without any physical contact with another guy," he said.

I was single at the time, and I knew I could definitely go two months without touching a guy, especially for two grand. I asked what I had to give him if I lost, and he said that I would have to clean his seven cars and his boat. He was obviously rich, but to me as a sixteen year old, $2,000 was a lot of money. We shook on it, and time went on.

I had a boy that really liked me at the time. I liked him too, and there were a few moments where we almost hugged, but I explained the bet.

"I like you, but I don't want to spend days cleaning cars and a boat. I can't have any physical contact for two months— hugs, holding hands, kissing, none of it," I told him. He thought it was strange, but thankfully he respected me.

It turns out my boss even sent people to spy on me to make sure that I was holding up my end of the deal. Of course I was. I was very motivated by the money, and I wanted to pay off my 1997 Saturn that I had bought for $4,000.

I held up my end of the deal, and my boss held up his. After two months, he paid me $2,000. I was stoked. Until this day, I've never been part of a bet like that. It was a bit strange, and some people might even say creepy, but hey, I won two grand.

You may wonder about the boy I liked...he started dating a friend of mine from high school, and they are happily married to this day.

Word List

server (noun) - a person who brings your food and drinks at a restaurant

bet (verb) - to make a bet; to risk losing something (such as money) if your guess about what will happen is wrong

single (adjective) - not in a committed relationship

grand (noun) - one thousand dollars

shake on (phrasal verb) - to shake hands to show agreement

strange (**adjective**) - weird or different

spy (**verb**) - to watch what someone is doing without them knowing

deal (**noun**) - an agreement between two or more people or groups

stoked (**adjective**) - very happy

creepy (**adjective**) - causing an unpleasant feeling of fear or unease

◆◆◆◆◆◆◆◆◆◆◆◆◆◆◆◆◆◆◆◆◆◆◆◆◆◆◆◆◆

Multiple Choice Quiz

1. How old was Camille when she started working at the Chinese restaurant?
A) 18
B) 20
C) 16
D) 25

2. What bet did the 30-year-old Chinese owner propose?
A) Racing cars
B) Going without talking to anyone for two months
C) Going without physical contact with a guy for two months
D) Eating spicy food for a month

3. What did Camille have to do for her boss if she lost the bet?
A) Give him $2,000
B) Clean his seven cars and boat
C) Quit her job
D) Buy him a gift

4. What motivated Camille to take the bet?
A) She wanted a promotion.
B) She wanted to learn Chinese.
C) She wanted to pay off her car.
D) She wanted to go on a vacation.

5. Who did Camille like?
A) A famous actor
B) The boss
C) A friend from high school
D) A co-worker

6. What did Camille and the person she liked almost do during the bet?
A) Skydive
B) Hike
C) Hug
D) Dance

7. How much time passed before Camille's boss gave her the money?
A) One year
B) Three weeks
C) Two months
D) Five days

8. How did the boss know if Camille was keeping her end of the deal?

A) He sent people to check on her.

B) He himself spied on her.

C) He asked Camille what she did.

D) It's not mentioned.

9. How much money did Camille win after completing the bet?

A) $1,000

B) $5,000

C) $2,000

D) $500

10. What happened to the person Camille liked after the bet?

A) They disappeared.

B) They married Camille.

C) They got a job at the restaurant.

D) They married a friend from high school.

Twenty

Snow

True story

I grew up in the Upper Peninsula of Michigan on Lake Superior. It is in a very northern part of the United States, with Canada on the other side of the lake. Weather up there is wild, and it isn't uncommon to see snow from October to May. We even went to school in blizzards. I have many memories trudging down my driveway through the knee-deep snow in my Sorel boots to catch the school bus at the end of the road.

My parents fully embraced the snow and all of the snow sports. Being native to the area, they were used to the heavy snowfall and long winters. We would go cross country skiing, down hill skiing, skating, snowshoeing and more. They even heated our house with wood that they chopped down in the summer.

One of my favorite childhood memories is being pulled behind the snowmobile on a toboggan. We had a long three-seater orange toboggan with blue seats. My sisters and I would bundle up in our snow gear and pile on the back of the toboggan. My dad would start up the snowmobile and attach the toboggan with a long rope. He would drive in our giant field of snow doing loops and circles trying to get us to fall off. We loved it. Sometimes we would fall off and the icy snow would go under our jackets and up our backs, melting against our skin. That was the not-so-fun part.

Afterwards we would always come inside and drink my mom's homemade hot chocolate with marshmallows as we tried to warm up. Sometimes she would have her homemade cookies or nisu, a traditional Finnish sweet bread, for us to snack on.

I'm glad my parents instilled a love for the outdoors in us. I learned that it doesn't matter how cold or snowy a place may be; if you have the right gear, it's possible to enjoy it. I wouldn't particularly choose to live in a snowy place like the Upper Peninsula, but the magical snow memories are always there to look back on.

◆◆◆◆◆◆◆◆◆◆◆◆◆◆◆◆◆◆◆◆◆◆◆◆◆◆◆◆◆◆◆

Word List

wild (adjective) - unpredictable

blizzard (noun) - extreme snowfall

trudge (verb) - to walk slowly with heavy steps

embrace (verb) - to welcome; to accept

chop (verb) - to cut

snowshoe (noun) - a special type of shoe made to walk on snow

memory (noun) - something you remember from your past

toboggan (noun) - sled

field (noun) - a wide open space

loop (noun) - curve

instill (verb) - to gradually but firmly establish an idea or attitude in a person's mind

◆◆◆◆◆◆◆◆◆◆◆◆◆◆◆◆◆◆◆◆◆◆◆◆◆◆◆◆◆◆◆◆◆◆◆◆◆◆

Multiple Choice Quiz

1. Where did Camille grow up?
A) Florida
B) California
C) Michigan
D) Alaska

2. Which lake did Camille grow up near?
A) Lake Michigan
B) Lake Erie
C) Lake Superior
D) Great Salt Lake

3. How long is the snowfall period in Camille's hometown?
A) October to May
B) December to February
C) June to September
D) November to March

4. What type of boots did Camille wear in the snow?

A) UGG boots

B) Rain boots

C) Sorel boots

D) Hiking boots

5. What did Camille's parents use to heat their house in the winter?

A) Electric heaters

B) Gas furnace

C) Wood

D) Central heating

6. What snow sports did Camille's family engage in?

A) Surfing

B) Snowmobiling, skiing, skating, snowshoeing

C) Waterskiing, hiking, golfing

D) Rock climbing and mountain biking

7. What color was the toboggan from Camille's childhood?

A) Red

B) Orange

C) Yellow

D) Green

8. How many seats did the toboggan have?

A) 1

B) 2

C) 3

D) 4

9. What did Camille's family do to warm up after riding the toboggan?

A) Made snow angels

B) Built a snowman

C) Drank hot chocolate

D) Had a snowball fight

10. What traditional Finnish sweet bread is mentioned in the story?

A) Baguette

B) Challah

C) Nisu

D) Brioche

Twenty-One

Learning How to Make Sourdough

True story

After months of traveling, we decided to settle in Portugal. Though I wasn't pregnant, I felt like I was nesting because I stocked up on all the spices and ingredients we had had in America. I missed cooking, so I decided to start baking sourdough bread. I've always enjoyed baking, but making sourdough bread brought baking to another level.

Sourdough uses a sourdough starter, which is a naturally fermented flour and water mixture. I had to make this from scratch because I didn't know anyone in the neighborhood that was into baking sourdough bread. I read up on how to make a sourdough starter, and then I gave it a go. It took three weeks of daily attention before my sourdough became active and ready to use. I quickly learned that making sourdough bread is both a science and an art. The first time I made it, my bread didn't really rise. I remember asking a friend for tips, and I watched loads of videos on YouTube. One time, the dough was like a soupy mixture. I decided to bake it anyway, kind of like a flatbread. It actually rose more than I expected, and though it wasn't pretty, it was edible.

Making sourdough is a process. The recipe only consists of four ingredients; a sourdough starter, salt, flour, and water. I meticulously weigh all the ingredients to a T on the kitchen scale. I follow all the steps—covering the dough, stretching the dough, folding the dough—but I'm still so insecure the whole way through. I've stuck to the same recipe the last few times, and it seems to make more sense than trying a variety of recipes. This way I can truly test the recipe. I have had the best luck with letting my bread rise overnight for about twelve hours. Every time I make sourdough, it is like an adventure. I've only made one really good loaf so far. I practice making sourdough bread weekly, but I think I need about a year or two of practice before I really become confident.

I honestly have wanted to throw in the towel a few times, but the satisfaction of mastering how to bake a perfect loaf outweighs my desire to quit. So I'll keep doing my best until I master a really beautiful loaf. If nothing else, it's been a very humbling learning journey for me.

Word List

nesting (noun) - the overwhelming desire to get your home ready for your new baby

stock up (phrasal verb) - to get a large quantity of something

ferment (verb) - to undergo fermentation (the chemical breakdown of a substance by yeast)

from scratch (idiom) - from the beginning; without using anything that already exists

give it a go (idiom) - to try something new

rise (verb) - to get taller

edible (adjective) - able to eat

meticulously (adverb) - very carefully

to a T (idiom) - to perfection; exactly right

insecure (adjective) - not confident

stick to (phrasal verb) - to continue doing something in the same way

loaf (noun) - an amount of bread that has been baked in a long, round, or square shape

throw in the towel (idiom) - to quit; to stop trying

master (verb) - to become an expert at something

humbling (adjective) - to cause someone to feel less important or proud

◆◆◆◆◆◆◆◆◆◆◆◆◆◆◆◆◆◆◆◆◆◆◆◆◆◆◆◆◆◆◆

Multiple Choice Quiz

1. Why did Camille feel like she was nesting in Portugal?

A) She was pregnant.

B) She stocked up on a lot of spices and ingredients.

C) She found a new home.

D) She started a bakery.

2. What is a sourdough starter?

A) A type of yeast

B) A naturally fermented mixture of flour and water

C) A pre-made bread mix

D) A kitchen appliance

3. How long did it take for Camille's sourdough starter to become active?

A) 1 week

B) 2 weeks

C) 3 weeks

D) 4 weeks

4. What did Camille learn about making sourdough bread?

A) It's an easy process.

B) It doesn't require daily attention.

C) It's both a science and an art.

D) It's better with a store-bought starter.

5. What happened the first time Camille made sourdough bread?

A) It rose perfectly.

B) It didn't rise much.

C) It became a soupy mixture.

D) It burned in the oven.

6. How long does Camille let the dough rise overnight?
A) 6 hours
B) 8 hours
C) 10 hours
D) 12 hours

7. How many ingredients are in the sourdough bread?
A) 3
B) 4
C) 5
D) 6

8. What makes Camille feel insecure during the bread-making process?
A) Lack of experience
B) It being new to her
C) Weighing ingredients
D) All of the above

9. How often does Camille practice making sourdough bread?
A) Daily
B) Weekly
C) Monthly
D) Yearly

10. What is Camille's attitude toward the sourdough baking journey?
A) Frustrated and ready to quit
B) Overconfident and ready to teach
C) Insecure but determined to master it
D) Indifferent and not committed

Twenty-Two

The BEST Breakfast We've Ever Had

True story

We are a breakfast family. Breakfast is one of our favorite meals of the day. We sometimes even make breakfast food such as pancakes for dinner. I don't particularly like going out to eat for breakfast. I prefer to eat it in the comfort of my own home, but first I always enjoy a good cup of black specialty coffee.

One particular morning, we were in Antalya, Türkiye. Our friend Anil said he wanted us to experience a traditional Turkish breakfast. He picked us up and took us to what was nicknamed "Breakfast Town" because there were so many breakfast places in this little town. We were in for a real treat because our table was up in a tree house.

When we got to the restaurant, we took off our shoes and sat on cushions on the floor. It was a very authentic place. Traditional Turkish breakfast always includes çay, a delicious Turkish black tea. Whenever I hear a spoon clinking, it takes me back to Türkiye in a heartbeat—people stirring their sugar cubes in little glass tea cups. Turkish breakfasts also consist of a huge variety of vegetables, such as tomatoes, olives, and cucumbers. There's also honey, jam, walnuts, and different cheeses. There are all sorts of pastries and breads, such as simit, pide, and borek. There are egg dishes like menemen. We let Anil order for us because we figured he knew best. We tried so many different kinds of food, and boy was it delicious. We ate to our hearts' content.

After we ate, Anil ordered fresh squeezed orange juice for the kids and Turkish coffee for us. I'm not a huge fan of Turkish coffee, but it was fun to turn our cups upside down after finishing the coffee and wait until a cool design showed up. Then we were supposed to look for little pictures in the design to tell us our fortunes.

When we were finished, we asked the staff to pack up the leftovers, and then we walked to the local market as our food digested. It will be hard to top this breakfast experience because both the ambience and the food were just incredible. Experiencing it with a local was the icing on the cake. It's definitely the best breakfast we have ever had.

◆◆◆◆◆◆◆◆◆◆◆◆◆◆◆◆◆◆◆◆◆◆◆◆◆◆◆◆◆◆◆◆

Word List

breakfast (**noun**)- the first meal of the day

pancake (**noun**)- a thin, flat, round cake that is made by cooking batter on both sides in a frying pan or on a hot surface

go out to eat (phrase) - to go to a restaurant to eat

speciality coffee (noun) - the highest quality of coffee available

nickname (noun) - a name given other than the original name

tree house (noun) - a house in a tree

cushion (noun) - a pillow for a seat

authentic (adjective) - not a copy; genuine

pastry (noun) - baked goods such as baklava

clink (verb) - to make or cause (something) to make a short, sharp sound that is made when glass or metal objects hit each other

in a heartbeat (idiom) - without delay or hesitation

boy was it delicious (expression) - used to say something was very tasty to one's

heart's content (idiom) - until one feels satisfied; as long or as much as one wants

fan (noun) - someone who admires something

fortune (noun) - a prediction of something going to happen in the future

pack up (phrasal verb) - to gather things together so that you can take them with you

ambience (noun) - the atmosphere of a place

icing on the cake (idiom) - something extra that makes a good thing even better

❖❖❖❖❖❖❖❖❖❖❖❖❖❖❖❖❖❖❖❖❖❖❖❖❖❖❖

Multiple Choice Quiz

1. Why does Camille prefer to have breakfast at home?
A) She doesn't like Turkish breakfast.
B) She enjoys the comfort of her own home.
C) She likes going to Breakfast Town.
D) She prefers dinner over breakfast.

2. What is special about the breakfast place in Breakfast Town in Antalya?
A) It's a traditional Turkish breakfast in a tree house.
B) It's known for its fancy decor.
C) It's the only breakfast place in town.
D) It's a fast-food breakfast joint.

3. What does a traditional Turkish breakfast include?
A) Pancakes and waffles
B) Sausages and bacon
C) A variety of vegetables, honey, jam, pastries, bread, cheeses, and more
D) Cereal and milk

4. What takes Camille back to Turkey?

A) Memories of friends

B) The sound of a spoon clinking

C) A Turkish breakfast song

D) The smell of Turkish spices

5. What is menemen?

A) A type of cheese

B) A vegetable salad

C) An egg dish

D) A pastry

6. What beverage did Anil order for the kids during breakfast?

A) Turkish coffee

B) Fresh squeezed orange juice

C) Çay (Turkish tea)

D) Specialty black coffee

7. What is Camille's opinion about Turkish coffee?

A) She loves it.

B) She doesn't have an opinion.

C) She enjoys it.

D) She's not a huge fan.

8. What interesting activity do they do after finishing their Turkish coffee?

A) Read a book

B) Look for fortune symbols in the cups' designs

C) Take a nap

D) Write a letter

9. **What drink did Anil order for the adults?**
A) Turkish tea
B) Specialty black coffee
C) Fresh squeezed orange juice
D) Turkish coffee

10. **What did the group do after the Turkish breakfast experience?**
A) Went back to the tree house
B) Walked in the local market
C) Visited another breakfast town
D) Had lunch at a fast-food joint

Twenty-Three

Starting Learn English with Camille

True story

It was 2020. I was studying Brazilian Portuguese, and we were also preparing to move to Galicia, Spain. Then the pandemic hit, so we decided not to move to Spain. This period of one and a half years was our longest stretch that we've had in our American home, and I was looking for an adventure. Maybe it was just a coincidence, but after a third person told me to start a YouTube channel, I couldn't ignore it anymore. I shared what people had told me with my husband Calvin.

"Maybe I'm running away from something that I'm meant to do," I said to him.

"We should pray," Calvin said. He specifically said, "God, if we are supposed to start a YouTube channel, send a Brazilian to confirm it."

Then we let it go, and I even forgot about it until a month later when my Brazilian friend José told me that I should start a YouTube channel.

"I think it's time," I told Calvin.

We jumped right in. I didn't have any experience; I just knew that I loved helping people learn English and that I wanted to do something with languages. We eventually started posting on other platforms, such as Tiktok, Instagram, and Facebook, where my videos have reached millions of followers; however, I've never gone viral on YouTube. To this day, my following on YouTube is small, but I decided to give it another go.

There is more work than I had ever imagined that goes into creating content, including planning, filming, editing, and posting. It wasn't until almost two years into having my social media pages that I realized "real life" English was my niche. I love thinking of creative ways to teach people everyday English. I often include my kids in my videos. Sometimes I have to bribe them with a piece of chocolate to get them to film with me, but they have fun filming, too.

Calvin and I never imagined the growth that would come from creating *Learn English with Camille* or the people we would meet along the way. I'm so grateful when I receive a message from someone telling me that my videos or books are helping them learn English. It is such an honor. Having a job I love is a gift, and I don't take it for granted.

Word List

hit (verb) - to happen suddenly

stretch (noun) - an amount of time

coincidence (noun) - a situation in which events happen at the same time in a way that is not planned or expected

ignore (verb) - to not give attention to something

pray (verb) - talk to God and listen to Him

let go (phrasal verb) - to not think about something; to forget about something

jump in (idiom) - to start something enthusiastically

viral (adjective) - spreading very quickly to many people especially through the Internet

niche (noun) - a specific area of focus

bribe (verb) - to try to get someone to do something by giving or promising something valuable

honor (noun) - a privilege

take for granted (idiom) - to fail to properly appreciate

Multiple Choice Quiz

1. Where were Camille and her family planning to move before the pandemic hit?

A) Galicia, Spain

B) Brazil

C) Portugal

D) Peru

2. What was Camille studying before the pandemic happened?

A) Spanish

B) French

C) Brazilian Portuguese

D) English

3. What was the longest amount of time Camille and her family had spent at home?

A) 11 months

B) 1.5 years

C) 2 years

D) 2.5 years

4. What did Camille's husband suggest they do before deciding to start a YouTube channel?

A) Move to Brazil

B) Start a TikTok account

C) Pray about it

D) Forget about it

5. How did the idea of starting a YouTube channel resurface after being forgotten?
A) A dream
B) A message from a friend
C) A suggestion from a follower
D) A successful move to Spain

6. Which social media platforms did Camille start posting on besides YouTube?
A) Twitter and TikTok
B) Twitter and LinkedIn
C) Instagram and TikTok
D) Snapchat and Pinterest

7. What did Camille realize her niche was after almost two years of creating content?
A) Teaching grammar rules
B) Vocabulary building
C) "Real life" English
D) Phonetics and pronunciation

8. How does Camille involve her kids in her videos?
A) She bribes them with chocolate.
B) She encourages them to speak Spanish.
C) She makes them moderators.
D) She edits them out of the videos.

9. What aspect of teaching English does Camille enjoy?

A) Testing grammar skills

B) Reading books

C) Creative teaching methods

D) Learning new languages

10. What is Camille's reaction to receiving messages about her impact on English learners?

A) Disinterest

B) Gratitude

C) Surprise

D) Frustration

Twenty-Four

A Brazilian Christmas

True story

We spent Christmas 2021 in Minas Gerais with our Brazilian friend José (the one who told me I should start a YouTube channel). Who would have thought that a language partner could become such a dear friend?

It was incredibly welcoming of José's family to invite us to their Christmas Eve celebration. The celebration started at 9:00 at night; I am pointing out the time because it's such a late start for Americans. Normally our kids are in bed by 8 pm. The start time of Jose's family celebration highlights one of the differences between our cultures. Our kids ended up falling asleep at Jose's family's house for a few hours, and we got back to our house at almost 2:00 am.

We love Christmas in America, and we are used to our traditions, which include decorating the house and putting up the Christmas tree. The majority of people who celebrate Christmas in America decorate and put up a tree; however, it's very mixed in Brazil. Not everyone who celebrates Christmas decorates or puts up a tree. José's family didn't put up a tree, but it was still a really special night. They were so thoughtful to buy our kids little presents, and they even bought a present for me, too. We ate a lot of Brazilian food, including ham, chicken salad, farofa and sweets, like brigadeiro and rabanada. Rabanada is similar to French toast and is delicious. Needless to say, I ate a lot of food and practiced a lot of Portuguese that night.

The next day, we drove an hour and a half to José's cousins' house. Their house was on a farm. The farm was quite stinky and gross, but we had fun. There were tractors, four wheelers, and a lot of animals, so I thought it would be a good idea to film a video there. I even milked a cow while we were there. The cow's milk was actually delicious and so fresh. José's family added some chocolate directly to the glass, so I got to have warm chocolate milk. I normally don't drink cow's milk, but I made an exception. My kids loved it and begged for more.

Other than exploring the farm, we mostly just hung out with a lot of José's extended family members. Later in the day, we took a hike up a beautiful green mountain and caught a lovely sunset overlooking the valley. We really enjoyed celebrating Christmas in Brazil, and we hope to do it again some day.

Word List

Christmas Eve (noun) - the evening before Christmas Day

end up (phrasal verb) - to reach or come to a place, condition, or situation that was not planned or expected

tradition (noun) - a way of thinking, behaving, or doing something that has been used by the people in a particular group, family, society, etc., for a long time

hang out (phrasal verb) - to spend time together

extended family members (noun) - a family that extends beyond the nuclear family, including grandparents, aunts, uncles, cousins, and other relatives

valley (noun) - a low area of land between hills or mountains

cow (noun) - a large animal that is raised by people

stinky (adjective) - having a very bad smell

gross (adjective) - disgusting

beg (verb) - to ask over and over

Multiple Choice Quiz

1. Where did Camille spend Christmas in 2021?
A) Minas Gerais
B) São Paulo
C) Rio de Janeiro
D) Bahia

2. Who hosted Camille's family during Christmas?

A) Calvin

B) José's family

C) José and his wife

D) Camille's parents

3. What time did the Christmas Eve celebration start?

A) Early evening

B) Late afternoon

C) 9 pm

D) Midnight

4. What surprised Camille about the timing of the Christmas Eve celebration?

A) José's family didn't celebrate Christmas Eve.

B) How early it started

C) How late it started

D) Camille's family had never seen a Christmas tree.

5. What does Camille's family typically do in America for Christmas?

A) Decorate the house and put up a Christmas tree

B) Go to bed early

C) Skip Christmas celebrations

D) Travel to Brazil

6. Did José's family put up a Christmas tree?

A) Yes

B) No

C) The story doesn't mention it.

D) They celebrated Christmas at Camille's house.

7. What kind of food did they eat during their Christmas Eve celebration in Brazil?

A) Pizza and burgers

B) Brigadeiro and rabanada

C) Sushi and ramen

D) Hamburger and fries

8. What is rabanada similar to?

A) Italian pasta

B) French toast

C) Japanese sushi

D) Brazilian barbecue

9. Where did they go on Christmas Day?

A) José's house

B) Camille's house

C) José's cousin's house

D) To a restaurant

10. What memorable activity did Camille do on Christmas Day?

A) Decorate a Christmas tree

B) Milk a cow

C) Open presents

D) Bake cookies

Twenty-Five

I Made the Tabloids in Peru

True story

Peru surprised us with its gorgeous landscapes and welcoming people. In my opinion, it's an underrated country with so much to offer, so I started posting some TikTok videos in Spanish. The videos I posted were interesting things that I noticed in Peru, like the long lines at the banks or the windows always being left down while people were driving. For each video, I would ask a question in Spanish and show what I saw. The Peruvians loved the videos, and several of the videos went viral. I gained around 60,000 followers in two months.

One of my American friends knew a Peruvian chef, and he told me that he had a great TikTok idea. "The chef can make three types of ceviche for you, and you can do a blind test and rate them. The ceviche will be from Peru, Chile, and Bolivia," he said. He was sure it would go viral.

"Sure, that'll be fun," I said. I didn't even give it much thought because I was excited for new content ideas.

To make a long story short, we did the taste test, and I chose the Chilean ceviche over the Peruvian, but I did say that the Peruvian one was also good. I even struggled to choose which one was the best! I got so much hate from Peruvians in the comments that I stopped reading them to protect my mental health. I also realized just how much Peruvians take pride in their food. To be fair, the hate was directed more at the chef than me. I was just an innocent taste tester. I also hadn't known about the rivalry between Chile and Peru.

Three months after leaving Peru, I woke up to some messages from my Peruvian friends with links to articles about me. Apparently the video was so controversial that it was shared in two tabloids in Peru. They called me a young influencer, which really made me happy.

In an effort to redeem myself, I decided to make another video where I tasted real ceviche in Peru saying I liked it. The video didn't go viral— of course. I still chuckle whenever I think of the story, and to this day, that TikTok video still gets comments on it every single week.

◆◆◆◆◆◆◆◆◆◆◆◆◆◆◆◆◆◆◆◆◆◆◆◆◆◆◆◆◆◆◆◆◆◆◆◆

Word List

landscape (noun) - the land that you see when looking out; mountains, rivers, etc.

underrated (adjective) - not rated or valued high enough

Peruvians (noun) - the people of Peru

viral (adjective) - spreading very quickly to many people especially through the Internet

ceviche (noun) - a dish of marinated raw fish or seafood

taste test (noun) - tasting small amounts of many types of foods to discover how they taste

hate (noun) - intense dislike for something or someone

pride (noun) - a feeling of deep pleasure from one's achievements

innocent (adjective) - not intended to cause harm or trouble; without fault

rivalry (noun) - a state or situation in which people or groups are competing with each other

controversial (adjective) - relating to or causing much discussion, disagreement, or argument

tabloid (noun) - a gossip magazine

redeem (verb) - to make (something that is bad, unpleasant, etc.) better or more acceptable

chuckle (verb) - to laugh

Multiple Choice Quiz

1. Where did Camille start posting TikTok videos in Spanish?

A) Mexico

B) Spain

C) Peru

D) Chile

2. What surprised Camille about Peru?

A) All the short lines at the banks and shops

B) Windows always open while people were driving

C) The welcoming people

D) The lack of interesting things

3. How many followers did Camille gain on TikTok in Peru?

A) 10,000

B) 30,000

C) 60,000

D) 100,000

4. What TikTok idea did the Peruvian chef have?

A) Exploring Peruvian landscapes

B) Having a blind taste test of different ceviches

C) Cooking traditional Peruvian dishes

D) Touring famous Peruvian restaurants

5. Which types of ceviche were part of the blind taste test?

A) Peruvian, Mexican, Bolivian

B) Peruvian, Chilean, Bolivian

C) Peruvian, Argentine, Brazilian

D) Peruvian, Colombian, Ecuadorian

6. What ceviche did Camille choose as the winner of the taste test?
A) Bolivian ceviche
B) Peruvian ceviche
C) Chilean ceviche
D) Mexican ceviche

7. What was the reaction to Camille's choice in the comments?
A) Support and agreement
B) Hate and controversy
C) Indifference
D) Celebration

8. Where did Camille receive hate comments directed at the chef?
A) In Mexico
B) In Spain
C) In Peru
D) In Chile

9. What did Camille do to protect her mental health?
A) Stopped making TikTok videos
B) Stopped reading hate comments
C) Deleted the controversial video
D) Apologized to the Peruvian chef

10. How did Camille try to redeem the situation after the controversy?
A) Apologized in a TikTok video
B) Tasted Peruvian ceviche and praised it
C) Deleted the controversial video
D) Ignored the entire situation

Twenty-Six

Caught

Lila was so mad. Her mom had grounded her for two weeks because of her bad grades. Lila couldn't help her bad grades. She hated school. She didn't understand why she had to take chemistry and algebra. She was a dancer. She knew that she was going to be a dancer when she got older.

She heard the ping of a rock on her window and glanced out. "What are you doing here?" She asked Kai as she opened the window.

Kai was her next door neighbor, sixteen just like her, and her best friend. Kai, on the other hand, loved chemistry and algebra. He wanted to be a scientist. Kai was trying to convince Lila to go skating even though he knew she was grounded.

"Come on, Lila. Everyone is going to be there. Aren't your parents out with their friends? We can come back before they do," he said.

Lila was so tired of being stuck in her room, and Kai made a good point. What harm could it cause? A few hours at the skatepark was just what she needed. She couldn't wait to feel the board beneath her feet and the sunshine on her face. She raced down the stairs two at a time and met Kai outside. They skated to the park together and had the most incredible time. Lila lost track of time and freaked out when Kai told her it was almost 9 pm.

They skated home as fast as possible. Lila's heart dropped when she saw lights on in her house. Her parents had made it home before her. She didn't bother sneaking in through her window but instead went through the front door. Her parents were sitting in the living room with disappointed looks on their faces.

"Lila, we are going to have to ground you for two more weeks," her mom said.

"It isn't fair. I hate this. I'm too old to be grounded," Lila responded, as she started to storm off to her room.

"You're only sixteen, and while you're under our roof, you need to abide by our rules," her dad stated.

Lila put her headphones on and blared her music, so she could drown out her parents' voices. She couldn't wait to graduate next year and move away for college.

◆◆◆◆◆◆◆◆◆◆◆◆◆◆◆◆◆◆◆◆◆◆◆◆◆◆◆◆◆◆◆◆◆

Word List

mad (adjective) - upset

grade (noun) - a number or letter that indicates how a student performed in a class or on a test

ping (noun) - a small sound

glance (verb) - to look

convince (verb) - to talk someone into doing something you want

grounded (adjective) - forbidden to leave the house (by your parents)

stuck (adjective) - unable to go anywhere

race (verb) - to go or move quickly

freak out (phrasal verb) - to panic

heart drops (idiom) - the sudden feeling of shock, fear, or surprise

sneak in (phrasal verb) - to try to enter a place without anyone knowing

disappointed (adjective) - unhappy because someone has behaved badly

storm off (phrasal verb) - to leave in a rude and an angry way

abide by (phrasal verb) - to accept; to follow a set of rules

drown out (phrasal verb) - to be loud enough to block out the sound of something else

Multiple Choice Quiz

1. Why was Lila grounded for two weeks?

A) She skipped school.

B) She was caught at a party.

C) She had bad grades.

D) She was disrespectful to her parents.

2. What is Lila's passion?

A) Chemistry

B) Algebra

C) Dancing

D) Skating

3. How did Kai try to persuade Lila to go skating?

A) He reminded her of her love for chemistry.

B) He mentioned a party at the skatepark.

C) He told her they could get back home before her parents did.

D) He offered to help her with algebra.

4. Where did Lila and Kai go to skate?

A) A school gym

B) The park

C) A shopping mall

D) A skateboarding competition

5. Why did Lila lose track of time at the skatepark?

A) She was busy with chemistry experiments.

B) She was engrossed in algebra problems.

C) She was enjoying the sunshine and skating.

D) She was at a dance practice.

6. How did Lila react when Kai told her it was almost 9 pm?

A) She panicked and rushed home.

B) She ignored him and kept skating.

C) She called her parents for permission to stay longer.

D) She decided to stay at the park longer.

7. Why did Lila's heart drop when she arrived home?

A) Her parents were angry with her.

B) She saw lights on in her house.

C) Kai was there with her parents.

D) She forgot her skateboard at the park.

8. How did Lila enter her house after skating?

A) Through her bedroom window

B) Through the back door

C) Through the front door

D) Through the garage

9. What was Lila's parents' reaction when she arrived home late?

A) They were understanding.

B) They were disappointed.

C) They were excited.

D) They were proud.

10. What is Lila looking forward to next year?

A) Graduating and going to college

B) Getting a job as a scientist

C) Starting a skateboarding team

D) Convincing her parents to let her dance professionally

Twenty-Seven

My First Job

TRUE STORY

Most American kids are encouraged to get a job around 16 years old. My parents instilled a hard work ethic at a young age in our household. We had weekly chores to do, and we didn't receive any allowance. I remember my indoor chores were dusting the living room and the staircase leading up to the second floor. My outdoor chores included helping water and weed the vegetable garden, mowing the lawn, and shoveling snow in the winter. I was also expected to keep my room tidy. My mom took care of the cooking and laundry, but I remember baking with her and helping her fold clothes.

My dad was a business owner of a first aid and safety supply company. We had a big warehouse located on our property as well as his work van. He would work Monday to Friday stocking companies' safety supplies. He built the business from the ground up. He was discouraged from starting the company by his own father, a poor pastor, because it was different from what his siblings did; however, my dad turned out to be quite successful. My mother helped with the office work and us kids helped stock his van and put away orders in the warehouse.

I started working for my dad at the young age of twelve years old; sometimes I only worked thirty minutes a day, but sometimes it was an hour. He paid me $5 an hour, which was big bucks for me. I remember getting off the school bus and going straight to the warehouse to get my job done. Working for my dad, I learned responsibility and how to manage both my money and my time. When I graduated high school at seventeen, I had saved up $10,000, which was largely credited to working for my dad a few hours every week. My four sisters and I all worked for my dad's business over the years. It was a blessing to have this job. I think part of my entrepreneurial spirit definitely comes from my dad.

Word List

instill (**verb**) - to gradually but firmly establish an idea or attitude in a person's mind

chore (**noun**) - a routine household task

allowance (**noun**) - a small amount of money that is regularly given to children by their parents

dust (**verb**) - to make (something) clean by brushing or wiping dirt and dust from the surface

tidy (**verb**) - to clean

warehouse (noun) - a large building where goods are stored

from the ground up (idiom) - from the very beginning; starting something from nothing

pastor (noun) - a minister of a Christian church

buck (noun) - money

entrepreneurial (adjective) - characterized by taking financial risks in hopes of making a profit

◆◆◆◆◆◆◆◆◆◆◆◆◆◆◆◆◆◆◆◆◆◆◆◆◆◆◆◆◆◆◆◆

Multiple Choice Quiz

1. At what age are most American kids encouraged to get a job, according to Camille?
A) 14 years old
B) 16 years old
C) 18 years old
D) 20 years old

2. What indoor chores did Camille have as a child?
A) Mowing the lawn
B) Dusting the living room
C) Watering the garden
D) Shoveling snow

3. How did Camille's parents encourage a strong work ethic in their household?

A) Giving a weekly allowance

B) Providing extravagant gifts

C) Assigning regular chores

D) Hiring a housekeeper

4. What was Camille's father's profession?

A) Chef

B) Pastor

C) Business owner

D) Gardener

5. Why did Camille's grandfather discourage her father from starting a company?

A) It was considered a dangerous job.

B) It was unconventional for the family.

C) Her father lacked the necessary skills.

D) The market was oversaturated.

6. What did Camille's mother contribute to the family business?

A) Stocking safety supplies

B) Doing office work

C) Shoveling snow

D) Mowing the lawn

7. At what age did Camille start working for her father?

A) 10 years old

B) 12 years old

C) 14 years old

D) 16 years old

8. How much did Camille's father pay her for the work at a young age?

A) $2 an hour

B) $5 an hour

C) $10 an hour

D) $15 an hour

9. What did Camille learn from working for her father?

A) Advanced mathematics

B) Responsibility and time management

C) Cooking skills

D) Interior design

10. What helped Camille have a strong entrepreneurial spirit?

A) Working for her father

B) Her mother's cooking lessons

C) Her education

D) Her siblings' influence

Twenty-Eight

Embarrassing Moment

Sandra had been practicing yoga for a few months. She loved the small studio just down the street from her house. She had a nice Monday, Wednesday, and Saturday class rhythm going. She always felt so rejuvenated and relaxed after a class. She was still a newbie, but that was okay with her. Everyone had to start somewhere. She had already noticed improvement in her flexibility, and her stress levels were noticeably lower since she joined the studio.

One afternoon after work, Sandra was starving, so she scarfed down some leftover beans and rice before grabbing her yoga mat and running out the door. She was about ten minutes into a yoga class when her stomach started feeling a little rumbly. There were six other women and three men in the room, plus the instructor. Sandra was in the middle at the back of the room. She tried to breathe through her stomach rumbling and focus on the instructor's voice walking them through a boat pose series.

"Okay, legs up, and let's pulse," the instructor said.

Suddenly a loud fart escaped Sandra's bottom before she could do anything to stop it. A few people turned around to look at where the sound had come from. Sandra wanted to crawl into a hole and die.

"I guess there's a motorboat in the class," one of the guys said jokingly.

Sandra knew if she didn't laugh, she would probably cry. She briefly imagined herself darting out of class never to return again. But all of a sudden, she lost control and burst out laughing.

"I knew I shouldn't have had those beans before coming in," she laughed, trying to keep things light.

Soon, the whole class had keeled over with laughter; even the instructor lost it. The awkward incident really bonded them, and from then on, she earned the nickname "Motorboat." She never ate beans before class again. She had learned her lesson the hard way.

❖❖❖❖❖❖❖❖❖❖❖❖❖❖❖❖❖❖❖❖❖❖❖❖❖❖❖❖❖❖

Word List

rhythm (noun) - a regular, repeated pattern

rejuvenated (adjective) - feeling full of energy or new strength

scarf down (phrasal verb) - to eat something quickly

rumbly (adjective) - causing a rumbling sound; unsettled

newbie (noun) - someone who is new to something

pulse (verb) - to do small repetitive movements

fart (noun) - flatulence; a release of gas

bottom (noun) - butt

dart out (phrasal verb) - to leave quickly

burst out (phrasal verb) - to begin (doing something) suddenly

light (adjective) - not serious

keel over (phrasal verb) - lean or fall over suddenly

lose it (idiom) - unable to control your emotions

bond (verb) - to bring together; to form a close relationship with someone

nickname (noun) - a name given to a person other than their real name

◆◆◆◆◆◆◆◆◆◆◆◆◆◆◆◆◆◆◆◆◆◆◆◆◆◆◆◆◆◆

Multiple Choice Quiz

1. How often does Sandra practice yoga?
A) Daily sessions
B) Monday, Wednesday, Saturday
C) Tuesday, Thursday, Saturday
D) Bi-weekly classes

2. How does Sandra usually feel after a yoga session?

A) Hungry

B) Tired

C) Rejuvenated and relaxed

D) Stressed

3. What did Sandra eat before the yoga class that day?

A) Pizza

B) Salad

C) Leftover beans and rice

D) Sandwich

4. What pose were they doing when Sandra's embarrassing moment occurred?

A) Downward Dog

B) Boat Pose

C) Warrior II

D) Child's Pose

5. How many people, including Sandra, were in the yoga class that day?

A) 4

B) 7

C) 9

D) 11

6. Where was Sandra positioned in the yoga class?

A) In the front row

B) In the middle at the back

C) Right next to the instructor

D) Outside the studio

7. How did Sandra react to the embarrassing incident?
A) She cried.
B) She laughed.
C) She walked out of the class.
D) She apologized to everyone.

8. What nickname did Sandra earn after the incident?
A) Bean Queen
B) Laughing Yogi
C) Motorboat
D) Yoga Joker

9. What did Sandra realize about her choice of a pre-yoga meal?
A) She should have eaten more beans.
B) She needed a heavier meal.
C) She should avoid beans before class.
D) Beans have no effect on her.

10. What lesson did Sandra learn from the incident?
A) Never laugh in yoga class.
B) Avoid drinking before yoga.
C) Don't take yoga too seriously.
D) Don't do yoga in a group.

Twenty-Nine

Our Worst EVER Airbnb guests

True Story

Let me start out by saying that 99% of our Airbnb guests are amazing. It's the 1% that causes the problems and leaves us with stories worth telling. We had a couple book our suite for two nights for Valentine's Day. I was out to lunch with my sister-in-law when the couple was ready to leave and checked out, so Calvin said he would clean our Airbnb. Most of our guests leave the suite fairly clean, and since the space isn't big, it normally takes us less than an hour to clean.

When Calvin walked into the closet after the Valentine's Day couple left, he smelled something funky. He looked around only to discover that one of our guests had pooped in our hamper in the closet. Yes, you read correctly: they had POOPED. There was poop under the extra towels AND on the floor. Calvin was utterly appalled and disgusted, and we had to get the space cleaned quickly because we had new guests coming later that day.

Calvin documented the evidence with photos, which we then sent to our guests, and he asked them for $200 extra to cover the hamper and towels that we had to replace as well as the extra time it took to clean and disinfect the space. We should have charged them $500 for how nasty it was. Our guests paid the fee without complaining but stated they had no idea that had happened. We wondered if they were so inebriated that one of them assumed the closet was a bathroom and the hamper was a toilet in the middle of the night. We're not sure what went on in there, but we hope to never have to encounter that again in our lives. It was absolutely the grossest thing we've ever had to clean.

◆◆◆◆◆◆◆◆◆◆◆◆◆◆◆◆◆◆◆◆◆◆◆◆◆◆◆◆◆◆

Word List

book (**verb**) - to reserve

Valentine's Day (**noun**) - a special holiday to celebrate love on February 14th

sister-in-law (**noun**) - the sister of your husband or wife

funky (**adjective**) - having a strange or unpleasant odor

hamper (**noun**) - a basket to store dirty clothes

appalled (**adjective**) - in complete shock; disgusted

evidence (**noun**) - something which shows that something else exists or is true

cover (**verb**) - to pay for

nasty (**adjective**) - extremely gross

encounter (**verb**) - to have or experience (problems, difficulties, etc.)

◆◆◆◆◆◆◆◆◆◆◆◆◆◆◆◆◆◆◆◆◆◆◆◆◆◆◆◆

Multiple Choice Quiz

1. What was the reason for the Airbnb guests' stay?
A) Anniversary celebration
B) Valentine's Day
C) Birthday party
D) Business trip

2. Who was responsible for cleaning the suite after the guests' departure?
A) Calvin
B) The guests
C) Siblings
D) Cleaning service

3. Why didn't Camille clean the Airbnb?
A) She didn't want to.
B) She was out of town.
C) She was with her sister-in-law.
D) She was taking care of her kids.

4. What did Calvin discover in the closet?

A) Extra towels

B) An unpleasant smell

C) Dirty dishes

D) A lost item

5. What had one of the guests done in the suite that caused the issue?

A) Spilled a drink

B) Left the lights on

C) Pooped in the hamper

D) Broken a window

6. How did Calvin react to the situation?

A) He laughed it off.

B) He was indifferent.

C) He was appalled and disgusted.

D) He was thankful for the experience.

7. How did the guests respond to Calvin's request for compensation?

A) Refused to pay

B) Paid without complaining

C) Demanded a discount

D) Left the Airbnb immediately

8. What did Calvin and Camille suspect might have been the cause of the incident?

A) Lack of towels

B) Intoxication

C) A broken closet

D) A miscommunication

9. How much did the guests ultimately pay for the additional cleaning and expenses?

A) $100

B) $200

C) $300

D) $500

10. How did Camille and Calvin feel about the situation and the cleanup?

A) Delighted

B) Disgusted and hoping to avoid a repeat

C) Grateful for the experience

D) Indifferent

Thirty

A Date to Remember

Marika's coworker Lucas had asked her out once already, but she had said no because she wasn't that interested. Lucas decided he was going to give it one more try. "If she says no, I won't bother her again," he said to himself.

"Fine, just ONE date," Marika agreed after Lucas brought up going out.

Lucas was thrilled. All he wanted was one date—that was it. Lucas knew Marika was the girl for him the moment that he laid eyes on her.

They met at Valentino, Marika's favorite Italian restaurant in their city. Lucas showed up with the cutest succulent plant telling her that it was for her desk at work. Marika accepted the gift with a smile. She ordered the mushroom risotto, and Lucas ordered the classic spaghetti dish. They shared tiramisu at the end of the meal. Marika was surprised by how easily their conversation flowed and by how much she laughed. This was not the annoying Lucas from work. He was actually interesting and very sweet.

The sun was starting to set when they stepped on the ferris wheel that overlooked the city below. They caught the most gorgeous sunset filled with purples and pinks, and when Lucas reached out to hold her hand, Marika was surprised to feel her heart skip a beat. She actually wanted to hold his hand. She was starting to see Lucas in a new light. How had she never noticed his cute little dimple when he smiled or his perfectly straight white teeth? Even his blue eyes seemed to sparkle under the starlit sky.

"What is coming over me?" she wondered. She had never in a million years considered dating Lucas, but now she couldn't deny that they had chemistry.

After the ferris wheel, they took a long walk down the main street in the city center. A lot of people were out because the weather was perfect. Marika wasn't sure what the future held with Lucas, but she was sure that this definitely wouldn't be their last date. In fact, she was the one who invited him on their next date. Lucas could only smile.

◆◆◆◆◆◆◆◆◆◆◆◆◆◆◆◆◆◆◆◆◆◆◆◆◆◆◆◆◆◆◆◆

Word List

coworker (noun) - someone you work with

bring up (phrasal verb) - to mention (something) when talking

thrilled (adjective) - very happy

succulent (noun) - a plant that stores water in its leaves or stems

annoying (adjective) - causing irritation

heart skips a beat (idiom) - used to say that someone is suddenly very surprised, excited, or nervous about something

come over (phrasal verb) - to affect (someone) in a sudden and strong way

deny (verb) - to refuse to admit the truth

◆◆◆◆◆◆◆◆◆◆◆◆◆◆◆◆◆◆◆◆◆◆◆◆◆◆◆◆◆◆◆◆

Multiple Choice Quiz

1. How many times did Lucas ask Marika out before she agreed to one date?
A) 2
B) 3
C) 5
D) 7

2. Where did Marika and Lucas decide to have their date?
A) A sushi restaurant
B) A burger joint
C) Valentino, an Italian restaurant
D) A vegetarian cafe

3. What gift did Lucas bring for Marika at the beginning of their date?

A) A bouquet of flowers
B) A box of chocolates
C) A cute succulent plant
D) A book

4. What dish did Marika order at the restaurant?

A) Spaghetti
B) Mushroom risotto
C) Tiramisu
D) Pizza

5. How did Marika feel about Lucas and their conversation during the date?

A) Bored
B) Annoyed
C) Surprised and pleased
D) Uncomfortable

6. Where did Marika and Lucas go after dinner to enjoy the view?

A) A rooftop bar
B) A park
C) A ferris wheel
D) A movie theater

7. What did Marika notice about Lucas during the sunset?

A) His new haircut
B) His cute little dimple
C) His choice of clothing
D) His watch

8. How did Marika feel when Lucas reached out to hold her hand?
A) Confused
B) Annoyed
C) Surprised but pleased
D) Uninterested

9. After the ferris wheel, where did Marika and Lucas take a long walk?
A) The beach
B) A quiet neighborhood
C) The city center
D) A botanical garden

10. Who initiated the idea of a next date?
A) Marika
B) Lucas
C) They both agreed on it.
D) It's not mentioned.

ANSWER KEY

1 Flash Flood 1. C) Dinner reservations at a restaurant 2. C) There was heavy rain and poor visibility. 3. A) Calvin 4. A) At work 5. B) Flip-flops, a garbage can, balls, and trash 6. B) Over an hour 7. C) The rising flood water 8. C) He was feeling under the weather. 9. D) They found a different route. 10. C) They were very surprised.

2 College Dilemma 1. B) She had pulled two all-nighters. 2. C) Her mom will be disappointed. 3. C) Finance 4. B) She doesn't know what she wants to study. 5. B) To improve her French language skills 6. B) Worried for her safety 7. B) Basic 8. B) Because it has a promising future 9. A) Changing her major 10. C) Espresso

3 Young and in Love 1. C) Handsome with piercing green eyes and curly brown locks 2. C) Three 3. B) Going sledding 4. B) In a science class 5. C) Hayden was in the same class. 6. B) Three weeks away 7. C) Her sister Claire 8. A) River Hill 9. B) Fresh baked gooey chocolate chip cookies 10. C) Worried and already planning to visit Sweden

4 Job Search 1. B) Radio station intern 2. B) To move out of his parents' house 3. C) Being a TV host 4. C) Three 5. B) Maine 6. B) One-year contract 7. B) Take the leap and go to New York 8. C) She is positive. 9. B) Sleeps on it 10. B) It is smooth and almost too good to be true.

5 Choosing to Live in Portugal 1. B) 8 months 2. B) They felt more alive overseas. 3. B) Having a European passport 4. B) They spoke Portuguese. 5. B) Access to a tax program with benefits 6. B) Randomly picking an Airbnb 7. C) They felt overwhelmed doing it themselves. 8. B) Opening a bank account 9. B) An hour north of Porto in a small beach town 10. C) Grateful and blessed

6 Adopting a Baby 1. B) They were expecting a baby. 2. C) Through adoption 3. B) They had warm eyes and kind smiles. 4. C) Elise 5. B) Excited 6. C) By red-eye flight 7. A) Miriam's mother 8. C) Carefully chosen baby outfits, pacifiers, and bottles 9. B) God's promise 10. C) Exhausted but thankful

7 Scammed 1. B) Tirana, Albania 2. A) It meant more income for travel. 3. C) He claimed his company would write them a check. 4. B) Travel 5. B) They hadn't received any form of payment. 6. A) Jan, the neighbor 7. B) The curtains were closed. 8. D) The story doesn't mention how. 9. C) $4,000 10. C) Never go outside of the Airbnb app for bookings.

8 Root Canal 1. B) He had a popcorn kernel stuck in his tooth. 2. C) It wasn't related to the popcorn kernel. 3. B) Advil didn't alleviate the pain. 4. C) He needed a root canal. 5. B) No. 6. C) Monthly payments 7. B) Numbness due to anesthesia 8. C) Have a milkshake 9. C) He was too numb. 10. D) Needing a crown

9 Speeding Ticket 1. B) Annoyance 2. A) It was cool 3. B) Her insurance would increase. 4. A) She didn't realize she was speeding. 5. B) She pleaded with him. 6. C) She was only going ten miles over. 7. B) Angry 8. B) Go to court and fight it 9. A) She told him not to worry. 10. C) Eating pizza

10 Rollerblading Mishaps 1. C) Rollerblading 2. A) Helmets and knee pads 3. A) Trying to get away from her sister 4. B) She didn't cry at all. 5. B) He thought Camille was strong. 6. C) 6 weeks 7. C)

She covered it with a plastic bag. 8. A) Right wrist 9. C) They signed it and thought it was cool. 10. B) Everything was healing well.

11 Beginning College 1. A) The college dorms 2. A) Sharon Stone 3. C) 5 4. B) Athletic achievement in volleyball 5. A) She wanted to focus on her studies and volleyball. 6. B) 30 minutes 7. C) A new laptop and clothes 8. B) 2 9. D) It was too much hassle and too expensive. 10. A) Her parents

12 Restored Hope 1. C) South Carolina 2. C) Pool shared with guests 3. B) He wanted to practice his photography skills. 4. C) Dominican 5. B) Big with dark skin 6. C) Camille had restored his hope in humanity. 7. C) Photography 8. B) Sadness 9. B) How Daniel had been treated poorly 10. B) Kindness always wins.

13 Rollerblading in Barcelona 1. C) Calvin wanted to settle down. 2. D) They adored the country. 3. B) They learned quickly. 4. B) Jumps and spins 5. D) The rollerblades were heavy and awkward. 6. C) Buses 7. B) Portugal 8. A) They were burned out from traveling. 9. B) Every week 10. D) Staying in Portugal

14 A Surprise Guest 1. B) He was tired from work. 2. B) Salmon with asparagus 3. A) He had a deadline to meet. 4. C) She was pregnant and tired. 5. C) His neighbor 6. A) Paris 7. C) He thought it would be fun 8. C) Increased his salary 9. B) She gave him a big hug. 10. B) Hiking and dinner

15 Bitten by a Weever Fish 1. C) At a beach in Türkiye 2. B) He got bitten by a weever fish. 3. C) 15 minutes 4. B) It was the worst pain of his life. 5. A) A jellyfish sting 6. C) A white vinegar soak 7. B) She threw up. 8. C) $35 USD 9. B) It can be a 10 out of 10 for the first two hours. 10. C) Bought water shoes

16 The Coolest Babysitter 1. C) 3 2. B) School counselor 3. B) Twice a week 4. C) $10 5. C) They were jumping on the couches. 6. C) Dropped an egg 7. B) Gingerbread cutout cookies 8. B) Work meeting 9. C) By carrying them 10. C) Built snowmen and a snow fort

17 Our Best Day in Italy 1. C) It's the cheapest month. 2. C) Searched online 3. C) 37 degrees Fahrenheit 4. B) Drove a rental car 5. B) To keep the springs a secret 6. C) Italian pasta, minestrone soup, and bread 7. C) To turn on the heat and warm up 8. D) Wine 9. C) Soak in the springs 10. B) In March or April

18 A Day at Sea 1. C) Snorkeling 2. B) Stormy weather 3. B) 20 minutes 4. B) Squids, turtles, colorful fish, octopus, and stingrays 5. B) Dolphins 6. B) Grilled fish and french fries 7. C) Exhilarated 8. C) An old class ring 9. D) Try to find the owner 10. C) Rusty but with a legible name

19 The Bet 1. C) 16 2. C) Going without physical contact with a guy for two months 3. B) Clean his seven cars and boat 4. C) She wanted to pay off her car. 5. C) A friend from high school 6. C) Hug 7. C) Two months 8. A) He sent people to check on her. 9. C) $2,000 10. D) They married a friend from high school.

20 Snow 1. C) Michigan 2. C) Lake Superior 3. A) October to May 4. C) Sorel boots 5. C) Wood 6. B) Snowmobiling, skiing, skating, snowshoeing 7. B) Orange 8. C) 3 9. C) Drank hot chocolate 10. C) Nisu

21 Learning how to make Sourdough 1. B) She stocked up on a lot of spices and ingredients. 2. B) A naturally fermented mixture of flour and water 3. C) 3 weeks 4. C) It's both a science and an art. 5. B) It didn't rise much. 6. D) 12 hours 7. B) 4 8. D) All of the above 9. B) Weekly 10. C) Insecure but determined to master it

22 The Best Breakfast we've ever had 1. B) She enjoys the comfort of her own home. 2. A) It's a traditional Turkish breakfast in a tree house. 3. C) Variety of vegetables, honey, jam, pastries, bread, cheeses, and more 4. B) The sound of a spoon clinking 5. C) An egg dish 6. B) Fresh squeezed orange juice 7. D) She's not a huge fan. 8. B) Look for fortune symbols in the cups' designs 9. D) Turkish coffee 10. B) Walked in the local market

23 Starting Learn English with Camille 1. A) Galicia, Spain 2. C) Brazilian Portuguese 3. B) 1.5 years 4. C) Pray about it 5. B) A message from a friend 6. C) Instagram and TikTok 7. C) "Real life" English 8. A) She bribes them with chocolate. 9. C) Creative teaching methods 10. B) Gratitude

24 A Brazilian Christmas 1. A) Minas Gerais 2. B) José's family 3. C) 9 pm 4. C) How late it started 5. A) Decorate the house and put up a Christmas tree 6. B) No 7. B) Brigadeiro and rabanada 8. B) French toast 9. C) José's cousin's house 10. B) Milk a cow

25 I made the Tabloids in Peru 1. C) Peru 2. B) Windows always open while people were driving 3. C) 60,000 4. B) Having a blind taste test of different ceviches 5. B) Peruvian, Chilean, Bolivian 6. C) Chilean ceviche 7. B) Hate and controversy 8. C) In Peru 9. B) Stopped reading hate comments 10. B) Tasted Peruvian ceviche and praised it

26 Caught 1. C) She had bad grades. 2. C) Dancing 3. C) He told her they could get back home before her parents did. 4. B) The park 5. C) She was enjoying the sunshine and skating. 6. A) She panicked and rushed home. 7. B) She saw lights on in her house. 8. C) Through the front door 9. B) They were disappointed. 10. A) Graduating and going to college

27 My First Job 1. B) 16 years old 2. B) Dusting the living room 3. C) Assigning regular chores 4. C) Business owner 5. B) It was unconventional for the family. 6. B) Doing office work 7. B) 12 years old 8. B) $5 an hour 9. B) Responsibility and time management 10. A) Working for her father

28 Embarrassing Moment 1. B) Monday, Wednesday, Saturday 2. C) Rejuvenated and relaxed 3. C) Leftover beans and rice 4. B) Boat Pose 5. D) 11 6. B) In the middle at the back 7. B) She laughed. 8. C) Motorboat 9. C) She should avoid beans before class. 10. C) Don't take yoga too seriously.

29 Our Worst Ever Airbnb Guests 1. B) Valentine's Day 2. A) Calvin 3. C) She was with her sister-in-law. 4. B) An unpleasant smell 5. C) Pooped in the hamper 6. C) He was appalled and disgusted. 7. B) Paid without complaining 8. B) Intoxication 9. B) $200 10. B) Disgusted and hoping to avoid a repeat

30 A Date to Remember 1. A) 2 2. C) Valentino, an Italian restaurant 3. C) A cute succulent plant 4. B) Mushroom risotto 5. C) Surprised and pleased 6. C) A ferris wheel 7. B) His cute little dimple 8. C) Surprised but pleased 9. C) The city center 10. A) Marika

WRITE YOUR OWN STORY

Continue Learning with Camille

4.95 / 5 stars
79 REVIEWS

My goal is to create practical & efficient English learning resources for you!

Keep learning with my real life English books, workshops and courses created just for you, the English learner.

www.learnenglishwithcamille.com

SCAN HERE TO KEEP LEARNING

About Camille

I'm a mom, polyglot, language content creator and world traveler having visited over 45 countries and 15 countries as a family. We love exploring cultures, castles, foods and languages!

You'll most likely find me studying a target language in a café somewhere around the world or exploring ruins with my family.

My language journey started with Spanish, then went to Italian, then Portuguese, French, and Turkish. I don't have a "gift of languages", but I learned HOW to learn a language! There are no shortcuts, but you can build positive mindsets and SM.A.R.T. language goals to learn quicker.

My goal is to help as many people as I can learn English and improve their lives through language learning. Languages have enriched my life and I know it will do the same for you!

Don't be a stranger, look me up on social media. I'd love to hear your thoughts on my books and content.

Tchau ciao!

~Camille

instagram.com/camillehanson

youtube.com/learnenglishwithcamille

amazon.com/stores/author/B09MDHZ596

tiktok.com/@learnenglishwithcamille

Printed in Great Britain
by Amazon